no more EXCUSES

eal life stories to inspire young minds to achieve

by SOTONYE DIRI

GW00640883

MINISTRY IN ART PUBLISHING
The Seal of Excellence

Ministry In Art Publishing Ltd
email: publishing@ministryinart.com
website: miapublishing.com

This publication is designed to provide accurate and authoritative information in regard to the subject matter covered. It is sold with the understanding that the publisher is not engaged in rendering legal, accounting, or other professional service.
If legal advice or other expert assistance is required, the services of a competent professional should be sought.

ISBN: 978-0-9560996-0-0

Cover Design: Ministry In Art Design
www.miadesign.com

Contents

Foreword from Dawn Butler MP

I became the 1st African-Caribbean female MP in British history to serve in the British government. The 1st female Minister of Jamaican descent and the 1st female MP in Brent and I am determined that I will not be the last.

I tried a few times to get selected and many people said, "Give up. There are not many black women in parliament for a reason", but I kept on trying and was finally elected to be MP for Brent South.

I became the 3rd black woman ever to be an MP on 05.05.2005, that day I will never forget. It made everything worthwhile; the sacrifices, the sweat and the tears.

This book is a book of hope, written by a young lady making a change. I hope that everyone reading this book will take every obstacle thrown in their way, put it in a box and stand on it, in order that they may become taller and reach their goals sooner.

I am sure this is the beginning of many untold stories. Together we can make a change......

Message from the Author

Welcome! My name is Sotonye Diri and I wrote this book just for YOU. I don't know how you got hold of 'No More Excuses' but I'm glad you did. I guarantee you that this book will change your life and open up your eyes to all the limitless possibilities out there for YOU. Don't just leave this book on the book shelf to collect dust or you will never really know the secrets to success, and could live a life of wasted potential and missed opportunities!!!

'No More Excuses' is not another text book, it's the answer to the £1,000,000 question everybody wants to know– How can I become successful? Well.... read this book and by the end of it, I guarantee that you will find the answer!

Over the last seven months I have interviewed 16 successful black British role models who were willing to share with you their secrets to success. They were very honoured to be considered as one of the 16 and promised not to hold back any information that would be crucial for your success.

Before I continue and let you in on their secrets, I must ask you two very important questions and I want you to be honest with yourself:

1. Are you always making excuses for not achieving your goals?
2. Are you happy being unsuccessful?

'The computer says NO'. That's right. In all my 23 years of living on this earth I have never once met anyone who is happy about always focusing on all the negative things in their life. Those that do, always say to me, 'Sotonye I want to change, I don't want to be like this anymore'. I then offer them the keys to help them transform themselves from an ugly duckling, always making excuses, into a strong, confident eagle, focused on getting things done!

Do you want to know how?.....Well it's all within this one book, 'No More Excuses'. You get to read firsthand the secret of how these 16 completely different role models became successful in their chosen careers; how they had a goal and made it happen, and how they did not settle for last place even though they may have started off at the bottom.

This book will prove to you that there really is a pattern for success that you can follow to make your dreams a reality. Success always leaves clues and it's your job to put those clues together from reading the stories of these inspirational and honest role models.

Positive role models are people who set a good example for us to follow. They are also honest about their past and the mistakes they have made along the way, hoping we will learn from them.

All of the role models in this book have had the chance to make EXCUSES but chose not to; instead they remained positive through their struggles and pushed on no matter what came their way. They decided to turn each mountain into a stepping stone and saw each obstacle as an opportunity to perform to their best ability, never once did they sit back and say, 'I CAN'T DO IT'.

These 16 role models decided they weren't going to let anything get in their way; not their skin tone, not their age, not their lack of qualifications, not even their criminal record. They saw each excuse as a hurdle that they either jumped over, went around, went under or just knocked out of the way.

One of my favorite sayings is, 'A man never drowns by simply falling into the water, he drowns by staying there'. The longer you keep making excuses, the longer you will stay down and out. Your mind will not allow you to think of ways to get out of your situation because you have told your mind to give up.

I once met a reformed mad man who told me a story about his life. He said, 'I used to keep walking around the same corner everyday and falling down the same hole each time until one day I did something different. I went around the corner, and jumped over the hole instead. When I thought differently, I acted differently and I got a different result'.

I call him reformed because only a mad man would do the same thing again and again and again, and expect to get a different outcome each time. Think about it, it's MAD behaviour!

You have the key to unlock the greatness that lies within you. Find the right key hole and push through those doors. The moment you start to believe in yourself, your life will change. You will no longer have any more time to be making excuses, you'll be too busy making things happen, winning awards, making lots of money and helping others become great!

So I ask you to get comfortable and allow the role models to take you on a very interesting journey. Don't just read their stories but learn from them. If you're serious about change and your future then let me be the first to congratulate you and to let you know that nothing is impossible.

ENJOY!!!!

NO MORE

EXCUSES

Ade Shokoya

One of the biggest achievements in my life was turning my life around, but the process turned out to be one of the hardest points of my life. I knew that if I wanted to be successful then I had to change my social circle. Some of my people hated on me for that, but now they wish they could be where I am today - a young black successful entrepreneur'

Early Years

I was born in the UK in East Ham and then we moved to Upton Park. I lived with both parents but for the first five years of my life I stayed with a nanny.

My dad was not around most of the time as he worked in Nigeria, but I never felt abandoned because he came to London at least three times a year. I also had a lot of uncles who looked after me and taught me how to be a man.

My parents were strict with me. They would always say, "Go and read your book," and when I was naughty they would get me to fetch my own beating stick. However, that did not stop me from getting up to mischief, which later got me into prison.

I used to get into a lot of trouble at school, always talking and messing about. Growing up, I used to steal stuff and play 'knock down ginger'. I was a young boy doing what young boys do. That said, I would say now don't be a fool, don't do anything that will jeopardise your future and don't put yourself out for your friends; it's not worth it.

Tricked

I got expelled a few times from primary school, which did not impress my parents. At the age of ten, I went to Nigeria for what was meant to be a two week holiday. I realised I was not coming back when my mum started to take me to see different schools in Nigeria.

My mum had to come back to London to tie up the financial side of things; the mortgage on 2 properties and my older brothers & sister's private school fees, with very little financial support from my dad. The stress became too much for her and she took ill and was unable to return to Nigeria.

At the time I felt like I was being punished but in hindsight, Nigeria was one of the best experiences of my life as it taught me about who I am, my culture, my heritage and how to be a man.

When I returned to England at the age of fourteen, I soon found out that it was not cool to have an African accent or to wear jack ups with white socks.
I never got bullied as I could always hold my own and after getting into a few fights, everyone soon knew I was a tough nut to crack.

Gang Life

At the age of sixteen, I left home as I did not get on with my dad. I left with the essentials- a mattress, a bowl, a spoon and a blanket. I went to stay in a mates' flat which had no electricity for a month. It was at this stage that I started to roll with the wrong crowd. I started stealing for survival and then it became a part of my everyday life. Eventually, all the furniture in the flat was stolen- the carpet, the plants, everything.

I used to hang outside Waltham Forest College, smoking and getting up to no good. Then one day a girl came up to me and said, "Why don't you just do a course seeing that you're always here" I thought, "true", so I enrolled for my A-Levels which took me a year longer than most to finish because I still wasn't that serious about my education or my future.

For nearly ten years I was seriously involved in gang life, which lead to me going to prison twice. My first sentence was in 1995 where I received a three year sentence for selling crack after completing college. My second sentence was for selling fake drugs after I had completed university in 2001 with a 1st class degree in Information Systems from Greenwich University.

I was strapped for cash and thought, "just this one last time" but I got caught. I gave a fake name and address but they already had my fingerprints on the database and I knew it would only be a matter of time before they caught me. I always knew I would be successful in life and did not want to have this incident catching up with me so I handed myself in to the police.

Prison Life

One of the worst things about prison was not even the conditions; it was the fact that I was never going to get back the time I had lost.

Being in prison the second time made me realise that this was not the life for me. I was an intelligent young man who just got a 1st class degree and here I was sitting in a cell with another man doing nothing. On both sentences I met people in prison who had been sentenced to life and they said they wished they could get back the time they had lost whilst in prison.

Having a criminal record is one of the most stupid things I've created in my life. It's so important that you think about the long term, your future. I knew I could excel in many things, I just wish I had never wasted so much time.

Opportunity

After serving my sentence I went to work for Car Land as I thought that that was the only job I could get with my criminal record. However, because I had been so willing to help others at University, one of my colleagues helped to get me onto a government financed graduate scheme. This scheme was reserved for the top 5% of University graduates in the country – and with my 1st class degree, I qualified.

I was required to go into a company that had no IT systems at all, analyse their business requirements, design and implement the necessary systems and train their staff on how to use them. The job was in Kent and I had to travel an hour and a half each way, driving a total of 140 miles to and from work everyday. Within the two year period I was there, I was able to increase the company's turnover by half a million pounds which was a big achievement.

At the end of my two year contract I then went to work with a large internet company, analysing and designing systems as a business/systems analyst. I was earning way over £35,000 a year but I was working long hours, usually from 7.00am to 11.00pm.

The day after I secured the company a £5 million contract with a large client, I was made 'redundant'. The real reason was because my department manager, a female, did not like me.

Blessing In Disguise - Genie Properties
To be honest, getting sacked was really a blessing in disguise as I was thinking of starting up my own property business. I had already been to seminars about property and was ready to go. So soon after in April of 2005, I started up my very own property business called Genie Properties with my then partner.

Genie Properties is a company that sources investment properties for investors at a good rate all over the world and shows clients how to build a profitable portfolio of fifteen properties in three years using little or none of their own money.

I went from earning a lot of money to just getting by when I first started up Genie Properties. I was working seven days a week, and sixteen hours a day. I had to make a lot of sacrifices. There were times when I had no money and I had to ask for help from family members to pay for my phone bill and other bills.

Being a very proud person this was extremely hard for me to do but I was willing to do what I needed to do because I believed in the success of my business.

Mentors
What also helped was having experienced mentors- people who were already doing what I wanted to do and making the money I wanted to make. I actively sought out mentors to get advice and to learn from.

If you really want to start up your own business, then a good starting point would be to work for someone else, get paid to learn all that you need to about the trade, become an expert, use all of their resources for free and then start out on your own. That's what smart people do. I've now started up an online business -www.itsanentrepreneursworld.com - that provides valuable personal development and business resources to entrepreneurs.

Before I started it up I hooked up with some millionaire marketing gurus, who became my mentors and are showing me the ropes.

Finding The Gap

You need to be able to identify what you're good at and what you enjoy, as your passion will get you through the hard times. Research the market, check if anyone else is doing it.

If not, then you need to make your product or business into a demand; something that will add value to people's lives. Put a proper plan together and then spend about six months testing it and making sure everything is tight.

Be determined and very persistent. I made sure I knew what I wanted, so that I would not be easily swayed by others or discouraged when people said 'No' to me. You can't be afraid of failure. You will make mistakes but just see it as one step closer to success.

Race Politics

As a black man living in a European country, my skin color may cause some small minded people to have stereotypical views about me but it really doesn't matter.

Look for people who want to work with you. If you have a product and the skills and you can add value to them then that's all that really matters.

When you start actively looking and learning, then you know that you are destined for greatness. Get inspired and stop making excuses. I never made any, so why should you? I continue to focus on my goals and give it 100%.

People only struggle with money because they think like most people. That's why 85% of the world's wealth is owned by 5% of the population. Become one of the 5% - a minority. It's time to think out of the box!

no more

eXcuses

Levi Roots

Its funny how I started out at Notting Hill Carnival, ended up going on TV and now I'm on the shelves in Sainsbury's and Subways. Who would have seen that one coming? Not me. I had gold dust in my hands for fifteen years before I realised that what I was looking for to make me rich was right in front of me.

Before, I had my music and my sauce and I was happy but now I have a cheque for the sum of 2.5 million bottles sold so far, now I'm really happy. In order to become successful you don't need to be a genius because I'm certainly not, you don't need to be white because I'm certainly not, but you do need to have a good plan, which I certainly have.

Now I'm known as that black man with the dreads who sings and has a wicked sauce

Life In Brixton

While I was in Jamaica my grandma taught me the magic of cooking. I then came over to England at the age of eleven. I was told that it was the land of milk and honey and gold - yeah right! My parents brought us over one by one, so I was the last to come.

We had a nice house in Brixton, but of course the area was rough, nothing like how it is now. The area was predominantly black so there wasn't much racism in the endz, however when I used to watch Tarzan, I knew that the black man would die because the media was always trying to put black people down but I ignored it and taught myself about being black and proud.

When I came to England I could not read or write because my grandma could not afford to pay for me to go to school. So when I did learn to read I enjoyed reading Shakespeare, I also used to write poetry but I was not a geek. I was one of the 'boyz' on road who liked to read.

I remember at the age of fifteen years old being caught by the police for stealing a T.V. They convicted me and I got a three month sentence at the Young Offenders Institute.

I thought I was cool but after spending three months inside, my attitude changed. I realised that I had so much talent inside of me and being locked up was just a complete waste of time. It was music I wanted to do; it was in my blood passed down from my grandma. So as soon as I had done my time, I went back to school and started up a little band.

From MC To Reggae Band

After secondary school I decided not to go on to college, it just wasn't for me. I left and started working as an engineer for Selbys, but after six months I left. Like I said, music was the only thing that got me excited! Now don't get me wrong, education is very important and it's good to study but for me, I knew what I wanted to do and staying at school would have delayed that.

I soon joined up with the great Sir Coxsone Sound System company. We were the first group who had a whole sound system, packed into one van, no one was doing this. We were the cool guys, everyone hated on us. We traveled with all our equipment to Birmingham, everywhere; we were like celebrities.

We were the first group to take our own sound system to Holland in 1980 and it was great, but it got to a point where five men in one group wasn't good. So I left to form my own band in the 80's called Matic, which was a reggae band.

I was inspired by the likes of Bob Marley as he spoke the truth and taught me about my history through music. I could not count on the history books in my school to give me an accurate account of my history so I found music to be my greatest teacher.

The only thing I knew about black people was that in every war film you knew the black person would get killed off first. As I grew up I started to realise that black people would have licked down Tarzan, and beat him up in real life.

I also learnt that we were a strong nation. I used to call Africans 'bubu' until I learnt that my ancestors were actually African. Knowing who I was, and where I was from, made me into a strong black man.

Grandmas Secret Recipe On Sale
When I started my reggae band I had left home but I was still very close to my mum. I knew how to make West Indian food from watching my mum and grandma cook. They never went to no cookery school, and neither did I, they just knew what tasted nice and used their eyes to weigh the ingredients. Cooking was natural for us and we worked together as a family to get the sauce out there.

At Notting Hill carnival we had a stand called Rasta'raunt where we would sell jerk chicken with the sauce. It wasn't until 2006 that I decided to bottle my grandma's secret recipe sauce and sell it separately from the dish. I called it 'Reggae Reggae Sauce'.

Dragons' Den
I was spotted at the World Food Market by a BBC researcher who invited me to go on Dragons' Den. At first I wanted to turn the invite down as I was not about to go on national TV and make a fool of myself, especially when my children told me that they "slay people on that show!"

After tossing the idea around in my head for a while, common sense finally kicked in and I said, "Yes". I had to take a dangerous route; it was very daring for me but I knew that if I didn't take the chance now I would miss out.

Being an entrepreneur is all about taking calculated risk; you weigh things up and then take action.

Before I went onto Dragons' Den I wasn't doing anything wrong in regards to my business; it's just that the right people did not know about me. I was known by my own people but no one had £50,000 to give to me. Some wanted to buy my sauce on credit, eat it, and pay later. I knew that it was time to expand my customers.

Sometimes I think back to the time the BBC approached me and I tried to go on stushy but I'm thankful that they did, otherwise I would still be the great Levi Roots who sells his sauce once a year at Notting Hill Carnival.

Dragons' Den transformed my image. I stopped looking like that guy who was going to steal your handbag and started to look like a respectable business man, even with my dreads.

Early Goals

It's important to think about business from an early age and plan for the long term. If you put money in the bank, the longer you leave it there, the more interest you have on it. So don't rush.

Things that happen over night end very quickly. You need to have long term goals for the next year at least. All successful people will tell you they have a plan of how they are going to make their millions over five years. Money does not grow on trees otherwise I would have been a millionaire long time. You make money through great ideas and great planning.

It's important to persevere and have a plan B when failure and doubt come knocking on your door. It's only by failing a few times that I soon became successful because I learnt from my past mistakes.

I could have given up on my business but I believed in my sauce. What made my business unique was the fact that I had a theme song called 'Put Music in your Food', which I performed on Dragons' Den; I was able to bring both my talents together, cooking and music.

I knew my idea was unique, but I didn't really know how much money it could make me. It took two white guys to invest in my business and grow it with me, not for me. Don't think I just sat back and took it all in. Everyday I was working hard, doing interviews, signing jars, I was everywhere at once.

History In The Making

It wasn't by luck that they gave me the money, the £50,000; I had to represent properly. The Dragons will never put their money into something just for fun; they need to see pound signs when they look at you and your product.

One of the investors said that they were very impressed with the way I presented myself. I went in there being me. If I had gone in any other way, it wouldn't have worked. I told them I didn't have a 100 page business plan, all that I had was my song which told them everything they needed to know about the sauce.

Going on Dragons' Den allowed me to pave the way for others. Now they have whole sections in supermarkets of Caribbean spices and sauces because of me. In Sainsbury's I continue to be one of the fastest selling products, overtaking Heinz tomato ketchup in each of the 600 stores and now my reggae reggae sauce is in Subway's.

If I can do it, then you can too. I have learnt how to appear more approachable and how not to scare people when I smile. A lot of Jamaicans think that everyone can speak Jamaican, so when a customer comes into the shop or restaurant, they say, "Whatcha want sir, some rice and pea der yea sir?" but not everyone can understand, so we need to fix up.

Becoming A Role Model

There are so many black entrepreneurs out there breaking through stereotypes. My only role models whilst growing up were those in the sports or music industry.

Now that I have been on national TV, I want the young people to see a black man talking about money and finance; I want them to be inspired to say, "It can be done."

In life there will be hard times and you may get rejected because not everyone can say 'yes', but just get back up, staying down just shows them that they have won.

Just The Beginning

I'm doing my thing now, and I have my children working in my restaurant, so I can say that I am a proud father who has brought change to the UK. I have helped to put Caribbean food and black people on the map of success and that's one of my proudest achievements, however I've just started, so England watch out!!!

Daniel Taylor

Who's the manager of this company?", "It's Daniel",
"You mean that black guy – he owns this company?
But he never said anything!"
That was one of the conversations I overheard about
myself and they were right. I never shout it from the
rooftops that I own such a successful interior
company. I'm here to transform a building and bring it
to life. Even though I am the managing director, I will
sweep the floor of my offices if I have to.

Being black does not make me better at my job and
neither does it stop me from doing my job. I've learnt
that if I work hard, have the right skills and do well for
he client, other companies will automatically want to
hire Metro Design Consultants

Jamaican Parents

Growing up in Battersea was cool; my family were not the richest family on the street but they understood the concept of value for money. We had one of those front-rooms with a lock and we were only allowed to go in there on special occasions. It had velvet-papered walls and lots of ornaments. If you were caught in that room, you better have had a good reason.

My parents were strict, respect was very important to them. I wouldn't dare tell my parents to shut up because I knew I would have had a ringing in my head for at least a week from their backhand.

My parents worked hard and that's what I admired about them. Even on a Sunday morning, a lie-in for my dad was only until 7.00 a.m.

My parents first rented a house before they bought their own property. In the first house all the children slept in the dining room, while my parents slept in the only bedroom. We had to move the dining table to the side and have our bunk beds in an L-shape. All my friends lived in similar conditions.

We used to play football on the streets - about twenty-five to thirty boys just having fun. My parents then decided when I was ten years old to send me to Jamaica. You should have seen the look on their faces when I told them I wanted to be a footballer; I was instantly on the next plane out to Jamaica.

'It's A Hard Knock Life For Us'

Jamaica was truly a shock and a half for me. Electricity was non – existent. One of the memorable times in Jamaica was when there was a wake because that meant there would be a 'cook-out' for the whole week.

Going to Jamaica really did change my attitude and outlook on life; I came back to England wanting to be the best. I was a lot more focused and money driven as I saw how hard my Grandparents had to work in Jamaica and I did not want to be poor, so I made sure I did well in my O and A-Level exams.

Climbing The Ladder Of Success

My first job was working for a printing press in Battersea. I even worked at McDonalds for a while. I always say, "If I lost all my fortune today I would happily go back and flip a burger if I had to, but I would prefer to manage the place".

There are so many people working in places like Primark who have the potential to be mangers but their goals and their ambitions are far too small.
I then went onto university and studied interior design at the Royal College

of Arts part-time whilst I was working at Westinghouse as a designer. Westinghouse was part of the US conglomerate, Westinghouse Electric, which owned a commercial interiors business.

At Westinghouse, I got promoted several times. I soon became the second in charge of the office furniture and design department for all our companies in Europe. The company was turning over about £60 million and I was traveling across the world, making deals, signing contracts.

Eventually the company got sold and it was at this point that I decided to go and do my own thing as my time was never MY time. I missed out on the early years of my son and daughter growing up, which really hurt.

Metro Design Consultants
Working for another company was great but working for myself was even better. I worked hard but I didn't have to slave at my desk because I already had the contacts I needed and the knowledge from running another company.

I started my own design and build company out of my bedroom in 1998. My business line was my home phone number. Metro's first ever job was for the U.S Embassy and we did well, after that there was no stopping Metro Design Consultants.

I believe that there are so many gifted designers out there who could go straight into business but I wouldn't advise it: build up your knowledge first, get to know people and gain contacts. As a young black man I knew I had to earn the respect of others and I did.

I did not come with attitude and expect to be given the job. I worked hard and proved myself. What set me apart in my career was being able to see the whole interior in my mind in a 3D format, and that's what clients appreciated.

No Excuses
One of Metro Design Consultants' biggest clients is a company called Boeing, the world's leading aerospace company and the largest manufacturer of commercial jetliners, military aircraft and missiles. This company was run by the great grandson of the Wright brothers.

Do you think I could have turned up to the meeting with my shirt all rumpled and my words mixed up? I had to present to them like my life depended on it and I won the contract.

I spoke a language at the meeting that they all understood not because I was selling out but because I needed them to understand what I was saying.

Just like Martin Luther King and Malcolm X when they were giving their speeches spoke English not slang, it's all about communicating to a wide spectrum of people, not just black people.

Signs

When I interview people, I can tell a lot about them from their C.V; the presentation of it, the language used and their personal presentation. There's absolutely no excuse for someone not being able to wear a suit to an interview. You can either get one from a charity shop or borrow one.

When I employ people I hire them for attitude but I train them for skills. When I look for employees I look for those with a commonsense approach and also those who can present their ideas with passion and confidence. A client must believe that you are a trusted pair of hands. I've never thought to myself, "I didn't get that contract because I'm black", if you're good then you're good, it does not come down to colour but skill.

Clients

Within the industry it is very rare to see someone like me, and even more surprising to see someone like me in charge, but if I can do it then so can you. All I had was an eye for detail and I was driven to succeed. I have now been able to work with so many amazing people and organisations.

I won a contract to design the buildings of Europe's largest black housing firm called Ujima, it showed that a black organisation did not have to look poor.

I've also designed buildings for the NHS, Disney, MTV, BBC, Lloyds TSB, the Conservative Party and so many more. Whenever you see a Conservative party member talking on the news from their main media presentation suite, the room they are using was designed by us.

What Every Interior Designer Should Know

Being great at what I do comes down to having an understanding of different software packages such as Excel, PowerPoint, Photoshop and AutoCAD.

Commercial interior design is also about being able to calculate costs. The client gives you a budget and you need to work within it, costing the materials, the staff, everything. So you need to know how to use the business package software to present all your calculations.

We are currently carrying out a £2 million project for a 999 call centre in Winchester. We have to make sure that this 999 centre has failsafe connections to other 999 call centres outside of the area in case there is a power cut, so we had to cost in the latest technology whilst keeping within their budget.

In this industry you have to show yourself to be the best. I remember one young man who was very persistent in wanting to work for Metro Designs. I turned him down but he still came back so I gave him a task to do within 48 hours. I told him that one of the bids to design a major interior had been rejected and I wanted him to redesign it for me. What he came back with was phenomenal, I called all the other designers into the office to have a look and I hired him on the spot.

My question to you is what sacrifices are you willing to make? What if someone says we have a job for you, but you'll be making tea for some of the day? Will you take it even if you have a degree or let pride get in the way? Isn't it better to be in there, than to be outside trying to get in?

The Sweet Smell Of Success

It's not an easy road but when you can walk by a building you have designed knowing that people are sitting in it and enjoying it, it's definitely worth it. I love what I do, that's why I now jump out of my bed and get excited about my day.

A New Way To Get In

Having a degree is good but the Creative and Cultural Skills Board, which I also work with, are looking for ways where young people can get a new certificate HND, a sort of apprenticeship.

Many young people are gifted, and it would be such a shame if the only barrier in the way of them fulfilling their dreams were their exams. So we're finding a new way to get more young people into the interior design industry because it's such a great career and industry to be in!

Dionne Jude

"You mean that girl who back in the day was known as Ragga Girl aka dancehall queen, and more recently as the Nappy Cakes Lady sold her products in Selfridges?"... "Well, if she can make it, anyone can!"

That's right, I stand here today not as someone who was born with a silver spoon in their mouth, but as someone who had a lot of passion and belief in themselves. The day I truly realised how much potential I had, was the day I became unstoppable

Identity

I was born in Preston in Lancashire, near Blackpool, and grew up with my dad's parents, who adopted me when I was one year old. I knew very little of my life before then so deep down I had feelings of rejection and abandonment which later affected my identity and potential.

My mum had me at a very young age, so I knew that she would never have been able to give me the life that my grandparents had. Even though I did not grow up with her, she still inspired me in so many ways.

My grandma was very strict with me, which often made me feel like she did not love me but I misunderstood her, it was 'tough' love, which we all need sometimes.

Despite this, in my teenage years I was a rebel with-out -a -cause. I thought I was a big woman who knew everything but boy was I wrong! Looking back now I can see that I was confused, searching for an identity and was full of hurt. I did not know that the way I was acting was a reflection of what I was trying to hide inside. I was really running away from having to deal with my feelings and emotions from the past.

Secondary school was a joke for me and I didn't do as well as I could have; allowing myself to be distracted by friends and boys. I bullied others as a result of being bullied in junior school. I was unable to love others because deep down I did not truly love myself. I was a very confident, powerful and assertive young lady but I did not know how to channel all of that in a positive way.

Golden Girl

While I was at college I was involved in the Dancehall scene. I used my creativity to make my own clothes and had the most outrageous hairstyles. I soon became known as the 'golden girl' because I always wore gold when I went out.

However, my raving and misbehaving nearly got me thrown out of college and I was advised by a senior member of staff to give up, and consider becoming a check out assistant. What he said really upset me but I tell you what, it was what I needed.

I wasn't stupid but I had been stupid. We all make mistakes but our misstakes are an opportunity to do something different next time or to find an alternative route to our dreams.

I was now determined to succeed. I stayed in college and passed my GCSE's and A-Levels. I then moved to London and went onto university, where I studied Sociology at Goldsmiths College University of London.

Independence

Going to university was my first time living in London and away from home. My grandparents had moved back to the Caribbean, so I knew I had to fend for myself in a big way. I really enjoyed my degree, and during my second year of university I panicked as I wasn't sure of what I was going to be doing when I finished university.

I knew I wanted to work with young people, but didn't want to teach or do youth work. I did some research and decided to do a post graduate diploma for a year that would allow me to become a careers adviser. I had to pay for this course, but I understood that in order for me to get somewhere in life, 'I' had to make it happen.

So I became a careers adviser but after just one year I wanted to do more. I then went onto work with pregnant school girls and teenage parents under sixteen and did that for three years working for the local authority which I absolutely loved, but I still wasn't 100% satisfied.

Nappy Cakes UK

One day I went to a baby show after having my first child and I was inspired to start up my very own business called Nappy Cakes UK. This was a baby's gift basket made up of nappies, toys and other useful items, in the shape of a cake. I won an award from the Federation of Black Women Business Owners, for Young Entrepreneur of the Year in 2005.

I had a lot of customers on-line and my product was being sold in Selfridges. I was doing very well for someone who had no experience of business; I literally taught myself.

I used to work in Selfridges whilst I was at Goldsmiths College, so walking into Selfridges to now see my product on the shelves for sale was amazing! You can only imagine the buzz I must have felt!!

When I originally approached Selfridges they told me they were not interested in my product. However being Miss Persistent and Determined, I didn't give up. I got some really valuable feedback from another company who told me to change some of the things that I had put into the basket.

This upset me at first but then I took a step back and made some changes. I sent the new and improved product back to Selfridges and they accepted it.

I learnt that listening to feedback was very important, and being determined, patient and courageous was the key to success.

Building Doors

In my life some doors have been shut but I have not allowed them to keep me down. If someone wanted to put a door up in my face, I would find another door to go through and if that door was shut I would then build my own door. I used to allow people's racist comments to get to me but as I grew older I realised that it was their problem. I knew I was a great person and I was very proud to walk with my head held high even when times got tough.

Starting up Nappy Cakes UK and maintaining it was very hard work, there were many times when I wanted to give it up and I also made a lot of mistakes.

My original motivation was the money, but I soon realised when there was little or no money, that I needed more to motivate me. I started to discover that passion and purpose were more important to me than the money.

Consultancy vs. Nappy Cakes UK

When I left my full-time job to run Nappy Cakes UK, I was head-hunted and asked to work as a consultant. I was asked to speak at many events, as people wanted to know how I was able to do it. A young, black, female who had no business experience!

As a consultant I started to make a lot more money from this than with Nappy Cakes UK, and all I needed was a telephone and a computer. It was at that point that I had to make a choice; whether to invest more time and money in my business taking on staff and premises, or to set up my own consultancy company.

In the end it came down to what I felt most passionate about. Whenever I helped someone through my consultancy I felt more fulfilled, it was a different sense of satisfaction. So in 2006, I stopped running Nappy Cakes UK and set up another great company.

Solid Foundations

Education had always been important to me and I knew the power of applying the skills I had learnt from education in my everyday life, so I decided to keep learning and took a few courses in Neuro-linguistic Programming, that would assist me with further empowering myself and others to fulfill their true potential.

This enabled me to expand my business into coaching and training and I named my company, 'Solid Foundations'.

I often ask my clients, "Are you able to walk in a straight line to your friends house and if a bus stop were to get in your way would you stop walking?" They often reply, "No, we would find a way around it". That's exactly what life is like; there will be barriers and obstacles in the way, but you just have to find a way around them!

I have made many sacrifices in my life and sometimes I have had to live on a few pounds a week with a daughter to feed and to take to school. Yet, I made those sacrifices because I believed in my dream and never once did I play the victim.

Finding Me

My greatest achievement has been identifying, exploring and moving beyond my own personal barriers by discovering the things from my past that prevented me from fulfilling my true potential.

I now have the experience, wisdom and skills to help other people to break through their limitations and negative mindsets, so they can live their dreams.

Being young is about enjoying life; it doesn't matter if you don't know what you want to do in the future, just keep taking small steps and see your experiences (both positive and negative) as a learning opportunity. Don't ever think that your past determines your future because it doesn't.

Wise Words

I have had some key people in my life like my grandparents, dance teacher, youth worker and certain teachers who were my role models. They were not afraid to tell me about myself and it was their wise words that motivated me to keep on track.

My journey from Dancehall Queen to where I am now has been a rocky road, but well worth it. I am now known as the 'golden girl' because like the singer Jill Scott sang, "I'm living my life like its Golden". I believe I am now living out my purpose; doing what I was born to do.

no more

eXcuses

Alexander Amosu

"There was a time in my past when I wasn't cool and people used to ignore me, I was the African boy in the corner of the lunch hall that no one ever noticed. Now when your phone rings you think of me.

I made my first million at the age of twenty four, and have gone from millions to millions over the years"

The Struggle

Growing up with my grandma in a council flat in Kilburn was an interesting experience. My brother and I used to sleep on the sitting room floor because my grandma slept in one of the rooms and her daughter had the other room.

My grandma was very strict and treated us like we were her house boys, cleaning the whole house from top to toe. We used to wear clothes from the charity shop and as a result I had no friends. No one wanted to talk to me because I didn't wear Nike, Adidas or designer clothes. It was more like Mercury or no name at all, just blank.

I remember at school I would eat lunch by myself. It was that bad that I didn't even get bullied, I was just invisible. I realised that the popular kids were the ones who wore the nice clothes so it was a challenge for me to fit into that group.

At the age of twelve I started to do a newspaper round, everyday I would get up at 6.00am, six days a week and get £10. This was not good in my day, it was child slavery; but I didn't care. I managed to save up to buy my first designer trainers for £50.00, they were Nike Air Max. I thought I was hot!

I was so excited I even wore them to school. That day I became Mr. Popular, no more eating by myself. Everyone wanted to know where I got my trainers from and that gave me power. I felt like the new kid.

When I saw the power of money I started to think, "How can I make £10 a day instead of £10 a week?" My mind was buzzing with ideas. I then thought to myself, "If I organise tournaments at my school, then I can get the students to pay to play".

I made about £1200 from the tournaments which I was pleased with, but I wanted more. I was now thinking, "How can I make this amount of money in one day?"

Role Models

My mind was on overload with ideas as I wanted that popularity. I had to feed and clothe myself, because my grandma was not going to give me money to buy designer clothes, neither was she going to give me business advice, so I needed someone else; a role model to guide me.

I decided to look to Richard Branson to learn from him. I saw him as someone who could inspire me and motivate me even though I could not speak to him.

Now a days', young people's role models are those that have nice cars, who hang in the estate. I had to find someone who challenged me, my thoughts and my actions. I knew what direction I wanted to go in and it wasn't the same as some of my other boys. However it was very difficult to find this kind of role model because there was no visible black business person in the media who I could relate to and copy.

If all I was doing was hanging on road and making a quick buck, and all I saw everyday was the same man down the road making quick money, then I would have related to him and my role model would then have become someone who was negative. However I wanted to make my millions legally and followed Richard Branson.

Business vs. University
For my GCSE's I didn't get very good grades. At college I studied BTEC engineering, a business start up course and retook my GCSE English. At the same time I was still on making money and started up a sound system and PA hire company earning about £250 per show. I also used to promote thirty seven parties a night, in total averaging around £2,000 per night.

I remember at the age of sixteen working at Tandy's, an electrical store, where I would make about £500 - £800 a month. I would then put some of that money into my projects and triple it.
I knew at this age that I wanted to be my own boss. I realised working for someone else meant I would not be able to make the money I wanted to make or have the freedom I wanted to have.

My parents of course wanted me to be an engineer. They didn't really understand this 'business ting'. I did not know what I wanted to do, so I did both. I studied and made my money, but later on one took over. At the age of nineteen I started up a cleaning company called 'Home Care Cleaning Agency' turning over £4,000 per month with a total of twelve clients. I got the initial funding from the Princes Trust.

At university I studied sound engineering and I was really enjoying it, until one day something happened that changed my life for good.

I found The Gold
I was in my room, messing around on my phone, composing a ring tone, when my little brother came into my room and heard it. He said, "That sounds heavy", and he wanted me to do it on his phone.

The next day, his phone rang in the classroom and the whole class went crazy, they all started asking him where he got that ring tone from. The next thing I knew, I had twenty one people on my doorstep begging me to give them the ring tone.

Now being a businessman I thought, "How can I profit from this?" That's right, I charged them £1 each for the ring tone and they were more than happy to pay: they knew it was a bargain.

I then thought, "Hold on, if I make ten more ring tones, and charge twenty one people £1 each then that would be £210". I then thought, "Actually I can make 100 ring tones, no, I can make 500 ring tones!"
So I did my research to see if anyone had done this before me, but I only found two people; one in Ireland and one in America, who only composed rock and pop. No one had tapped into the urban music ring tone market.

At that point, all I saw were the pound signs in my eyes. I was about to tap into a market where there was a huge gap and I was going to fill it. I made a bold decision to leave university and turn my skill into a business.

R'n'B Ring Tones
In the first year of setting up R'n'B Ring Tones, I made £1.6 million. I was very surprised when my accountant told me, I thought he was lying. I even had to go down and see him to check it out and he was right. Within the next four years I made £6.3 million. I then sold R'n'B Ring Tones for just under £9 million in 2004 as the market was getting fierce. I knew it was only a matter of time before people started copying me, so I had an exit strategy where I could still get out with a bit of money under my belt.

So by the age of twenty four, I was a millionaire. Did I change? Well, I tried not to. I even stayed in the same 'endz' but, when someone tried to steal my car I knew it was time to move out.

From a young age I have had to make many sacrifices to get to where I am today; the millions of pounds I have accumulated over the years didn't just fall into my lap. When my boys were out partying, I was in the house working hard, thinking of next businesses to start up. Was it worth it? Yes because they are still paying to get into parties, I just walk in.

More Businesses
I now have two more brilliant phone businesses. One called Mobs Video, which allows you to access and download videos direct to your phone. The other business involves us making customised phones in gold, white gold and various colours of diamonds. These phones can be bought in Selfridges and Harvey Nichols.

It's all about finding a gap in the market and going for it before anyone else does.

There will come a time when you will need to show your portfolio to investors and companies when trying to get your product into their shop.

My portfolio shows people, 'if I have done it in the past, I can do it again'. It contains a few press releases, figures of past achievements and awards I have won. Out of fear of missing out on a good product the shops will probably take a chance on you but only on the basis that there is a demand for your product.

Household Name

The fact that I don't want to be poor is what drives me to keep coming up with brilliant ideas. I want to have an entire empire. I want 'Amosu' to be a household name just like Russell Simmons and Richard Branson.

I was four months away from finishing university before I left. I told my teacher that I was coming back, I haven't been back since. Some people ask me, "Why didn't you just complete university?"

Well, I saw the opportunity to become rich and I took it. For me if I was going to do this ring tone business then it had to work.

Once I've decided I'm going for it, I will make it because I'm not going back to sleeping on the floor and wearing clothes from charity shops.

Knowledge + Self Belief + Skill + Passion = Success

The business course I studied at college really helped me to understand the basics of business. If you want to be the best athlete in the world, but you don't know how to sprint, people will laugh at you; it's the same with business. You must have at least the basic knowledge to save yourself from making time wasting mistakes.

Never give up and always believe in yourself. In my world, money has the power not colour. Never put yourself into a situation where you don't achieve your dreams. If you don't try something then you have failed yourself.

A business plan is no good without implementation, planning and knowledge. Find out what motivates you and use that as a tool to keep you going. Success is easier to come by if you're doing something you're good at and enjoy.

I've achieved only a few of my dreams, so I won't stop until I've built my entire empire and more. Personally I don't think I've even done much.

no more

eXcuses

Tony Cesay

"Commonwealth and National ABA Champion Boxer. So many people washed their hands of me and thought I was going to amount to nothing, but I knew where my strength was. I didn't allow the negativity to get me down or to keep me on the streets; I became a champion, boxing all around the world.

My boxing career was great! It took only one person to believe in me, and that was myself; I had to tell myself I was a champion long before I even fought my first fight. Now that I've hung up my boxing gloves, I can still say I'm a champion today because I'm changing the lives of young people in London and Sierra Leone by bringing out the champion in them"

Playing Mum And Dad

I grew up in Stepney Green with both parents, but they were not around a lot of the time as my dad was studying and my mum had her own business in Sierra Leone, so I had to play mum and dad to my younger siblings.

From the age of six I knew how to iron my own clothes and by the age of eleven I knew how to plait hair. There were times when we used to live on bread and sugar because there was no money to buy any food.

We lived in a very poor area, in a council house with four bedrooms. There were seven of us in total, so we had to share the bedrooms. I respected my parents while I was growing up but after a while I soon wanted to make my own decisions and go down my own path. They tried to correct me and teach me but I thought I knew it all. I wish I had listened to them because if I had, I probably would have been more successful at an earlier age.

I was one of the worst behaved kids at school. I saw school as my release; a time where I didn't have to look after anyone. The teachers found me very difficult to manage. One time I locked my teacher in the cupboard during a detention and went home, it was the cleaner who let her out. I thought it was so funny and so did all my friends, but really it was very silly and dangerous.

At school I never really got into any real trouble as the teachers loved me. They found me very funny and I only got suspended once for two days. I was quite good at English and P.E and those were the only two GCSE's I got which was useful when I went on to study Leisure and Recreation at college.

My Drive

I remember at school the headmaster calling me into his office and telling me that I was good with my hands, but I would never be a scientist or a doctor, as I didn't have the brains. I wanted to prove him wrong. I didn't want to be a doctor but I sure wasn't going to be a failure. What he said made me even more determined to succeed.

Champion Boxer

Whilst I was at school I wanted to be a footballer. At the age of fifteen I used to coach little kids from Stepney Green Council and I used to play semi professional football for Millwall, Charlton, Bournemouth, Sweden and Swansea; however I never had enough discipline and a little injury ended my career.

I then got interested in boxing. This was a good sport for me as I had a lot of anger inside of me, so boxing allowed me to vent that anger in a controlled way and stopped me from getting arrested because I was no longer fighting on road but in the ring.

"Whose There?"

One day I was eating fish and chips and the door of a gym flew open. I was so nosey that I went inside to see what was happening. A guy called Freddy who was the coach said, "Come in, come and hit this bag!" so I did. He then said to me, "Are you coming back next week?" so I did and I kept on going back.

I told them at the club, that I was going to become a champion and they all laughed at me. Little did they know that I was to become the first champion in that club. I won the 'Novice Championships' for beginners and the PLA's whilst I was there.

I then left to go to 'The Repton Boys' boxing club. This club was for the big boys; those that wanted to make it big in the boxing world. It was there that I learnt the whole trade of boxing and I became a bigger champion. I wanted to better myself, so I was at the right place.
Repton Boys was a brilliant school as it had a good system of coaches and a good foundation for boxing.

A few years later, I won the 'London Championship' at the age of twenty four and the 'ABA' National Title. I got to travel the world and it changed my life. Traveling and winning games expanded my mind to life outside of the estates.

My History - Education

I started to learn about where I was from; my history. I learnt that my people were strong and that they were fighters. If I had known this from an earlier age, life would have been very different for me because I would have been empowered to want to be successful much earlier.
I only found out about people like Martin Luther King when I was twenty years old.

Knowing your history is important but so is being educated academically so that you can come out of poverty.
Boxing taught me how to be more disciplined and made me into a confident person. I stopped hanging on road and became focused.

The moment I changed my friends and started rolling with positive people, I became free to be who I wanted to be, to achieve my dreams and goals. The people at Repton Boys wanted to be the best and that attitude rubbed off on me.

Simply The Best

Boxing became my everything; I used to work in the morning for Royal Mail and then go boxing in the evening every day. I was on this boxing thing hard, I simply wanted to be the best.

If I went out clubbing with all my football friends and boxing friends, I would leave at a certain time because I had training in the morning. I didn't smoke or drink because I wanted my fitness levels to be on point.

During my boxing career I was fortunate to meet the great Muhammad Ali twice; He was one of my role models. What I loved about him was that he knew how to scare his opponents without even throwing any punches. He used to shout loud and also declare he was the 'winner' before he entered the ring, and he did win.

Boxing is all about putting fear into your opponents mind; psyching them out mentally.

To become a great boxer you need to have speed, power, great footwork and good balance co-ordination. You also need to develop your twitch muscles, so you can have quick reflexes.

I had all of these and that's why I won a lot of my fights. Sometimes I did lose but I never gave up. Winning made me feel like I was on top of the world, but when I lost, it made me even more determined to win my next fight. I would train harder; pushing myself beyond my limits.

Invincible
I never once thought to myself, "What if I get injured, or boxed in my head several times?" I had to be fearless. I was able to build up this attitude and confidence through training hard and developing my skills and techniques.

I always strived to be the best and I soon became bigger than a lot of the teachers who tried to put me down. I won the gold and bronze Commonwealth Cup; the gold and silver Greece Cup; a gold and silver medal in Denmark; the Finland Cup and so many more other medals.

I boxed for about twenty years before I finally gave it up. I felt that it was time for me to train up the next generation of boxing hopefuls. I wanted to teach them everything I knew, so in 2000 I started up my very own boxing academy called 'Omnibus Kids Glove' for kids from deprived areas or disadvantaged backgrounds.

The Next Generation
The success of 'Omnibus Kids Glove' has been down to the fact that I talk to the kids on the level. I don't just teach them how to box but we look at the reality of their life and the choices they're making. I teach them about confidence and about having high self esteem. The Queen was so impressed with my work that she awarded me an OBE award for my services to the community.

There was one boy who came to train in my gym from Hackney who was caught up in gangs and drugs but once he started to train with me, his life changed.

He no longer hangs around with his negative friends or hangs on the street because everyday he's at the gym; focused, wanting to be the best boxer. It's all about the get up and go attitude. If you want it then it's yours, but what are you willing to do or give up to get it?

I'm now building a sports academy in Sierra Leone. This is what really keeps me going, the fact that I can bring change and influence to my own country. Even though I'm in England and I've won lots of medals, my proudest moment will be seeing one of the young people trained up in my academy in Sierra Leone in the World Olympics.

I have to say that I'm proud of my achievements so far. I've learnt that people will always try to label you but at the end of the day it comes down to what you call yourself. I knew I was a champion from day; I was just waiting for the rest of the world to catch on.

Dreams Can Come True

When you know who you are you can empower those around you; your friends and family. If you take on the negativity of your society, then you will pass it onto your kids and they will then pass it onto their kids, and so on.

You need to hang around with positive people; people who want to fly to the moon or be the next prime minister, because they will motivate you to dream big.

There are so many people out there who can help you. To get into boxing visit your local gym and find a mentor, watch boxing on the TV, get interested in it and you never know - you could be the next Muhammad Ali.

If you've got any ambition or dreams don't give up on them because 'dreams keep you alive'.

Dawn Butler

became the 1st African-Caribbean female MP in British history to serve in the British government. The 1st female Minister of Jamaican descent and the 1st female MP in Brent and I am determined that I will not be the last.

I tried a few times to get selected and many people said, "Give up. There are not many black women in parliament for a reason", but I kept on trying and was finally elected to be MP for Brent South.

I became the 3rd black woman ever to be an MP on 05.05.2005, that day I will never forget. It made everything worthwhile; the sacrifices, the sweat and the tears

Parents As Role Models

Parents As Role Models
I guess that attitude of never giving up was instilled in me from an early age when my teachers did not believe in me. In fact, I remember completing my history homework with such care and precision, that when my teacher read it she said, "It's too good to be your work," and gave me a D for cheating!

Determination was taught to me by my very own parents who came to London when black people had nothing to their name, only hope and dreams and a promise of a better life. My parents worked hard rising above the prejudices and left legacies for us to follow.

My dad worked all night as an engineer for the railway and my mum was a nurse. Journalists have said I was poor, I think they have their priorities wrong; I was never poor. There was always plenty of food in our house and clothes on my back; bearing in mind I had four brothers and a sister I kind of resent that terminology.

I suppose I didn't have designer clothes and the latest gadgets, but is that really what's important? I must admit that when my mum used to make some of my clothes I hated it but how things change, I would love for her to make some outfits for me now, or make me a dress out of the Jamaican flag.

My Upbringing

My mum was one of those extremely strict parents. I wasn't allowed to carry a see through plastic bag (scandal bag) around with me or eat on the street as it was seen as a sign of disrespect and people would think I was homeless. Can you imagine that ethos now? With all the chicken and chip shops everywhere.

This typical Jamaican upbringing did shape me into who I am today; disciplined and hard working. I remember when I used to have to be up from 6.00am and work till 8.00pm in my parent's bakery at the age of fourteen.

Walthamstow Market

Before working at my parent's bakery I worked in Walthamstow market, where I used to sell bras and knickers from 4.00am to 6.00pm. For an extra 50p I would help set up the stall next door. I used to get £5.00 a day and then I got a pay rise where my salary went up to £7.50 a day.

In those days that was a lot of money, especially when my pocket money was around 50p a week. I loved being financially independent with my £7.50 and told my parents to stop giving me pocket money.

Good Teachers vs. Bad Teachers

My school was very diverse. When the film 'Roots' came out, there were so many fights because people would call you names, demand you act like a slave and other foolish things like that. School was hard, not because of the racism and fights; it was much deeper than that. I almost left school because I felt some teachers didn't believe in me.

I wanted to be a lawyer, but my teachers told me to be realistic. They wanted me to be a runner because I was fast and could win medals for the school. I promptly gave up running. The only teacher who really encouraged me was my I.C.T teacher; I guess that was one of the reasons why I studied computers at Waltham Forest College as homage to my teacher, Mr. Taylor.

Money, Money, Money

When I finished college, I had planned to go to university, but after a discussion with some friends we decided it would be wise to test the job market. I was a pretty good programmer so the thought of getting a good job and earning money for a little while before continuing study appealed to me.

So I set myself a high wage rate and tested the job market, I was successful at the first job I applied for; that of a Systems Analyst for Johnson Matthey. I was well paid and still living at home, so I saved a little and spent a lot, bought my mum expensive things every payday and treated myself to a convertible, expensive shoes, designer clothes and went on holidays; but there was something missing.

My True Passion

I had previously run an after school club and I began to organise different show cases to raise money for various charities such as sickle cell. I also raised money to send a young boy with cerebral palsy to the Pedro Institution in Hungary. It was then I realised my true enjoyment came from helping others.

In Johnson Matthey I was working in a very male dominated industry where I suffered sexual harassment, so when the opportunity came up for me to take redundancy, I left.

I took some time to pursue my charity work, and then I started working for the Employment service where at a young age I was managing a team of twelve; many of whom were older than me. I then worked full time for the Trade Union movement, where I started to help those who had been treated unfairly at work. This also gave me the opportunity to study Employment Law and various other qualifications.

The Right Attitude

As a Trade Union official, I will always remember when I won my first court case and remember the words of the teacher who tried to discourage me from being a lawyer. People will always have something negative to say about you, but that's their opinion and there's no reason why you have to take their views on board. Having that attitude was something that definitely helped me to persevere when I encountered racism in the least likely of places; the Houses of Parliament.

Becoming An MP

The thought of becoming an MP was a desire that developed over time. I wasn't a career politician and there was so much negative press around politicians, I wasn't sure if it was really worth all the hassle.

To become an MP, you need to wait for a seat to become available, and then you express your interest. That's the easiest part, the next step is to send your CV to every single Labour Party member, and some can range from 200 to 1,000+ members. You have to persuade the members to choose you. They have to believe you genuinely have a passion and desire to see the lives of the community transformed.

Getting into parliament was not easy at all. The first rejection was disappointing but cool, the second rejection I thought, "Ok, I'm still standing", but the third time round, I wasn't taking no for an answer. I worked harder than I ever had; going out onto the streets, visiting every single party member and explaining my vision for Brent.

Sacrifices I Had To Make

During my campaign I had no time off, I cancelled two long awaited trips to Jamaica, lost two stones in weight and never slept. I spent money on leaflets promoting who I was and my vision. Some people asked, 'Why don't you just give up?' The thing is, I don't like to be over-dramatic, but if the slaves had given up fighting, I would not be free.

I saw every obstacle as a stepping stone to reach my next goal. I believe that nothing should stop you in this world from trying except death.

Characteristics Of An MP

To become a great MP, I believe you need to have a vision, and believe in your talent and strengths. You also need to work very hard and ultimately persuade people to vote for you. Taking risks stretches you beyond your own imagination. I became successful because I worked hard, I was committed, and I had the ability to change and create.

Parliament is not a place for making money and having fun, it's about your passion. I'm a hard worker but I've worked harder than any other time in my life, and when I walk the streets of Brent, I know it's worth it.

I hope that I am leaving a legacy for others to follow just like my parents have left for me.

'I Will Not Give Up'

There are people in Brent, mainly the Lib Dems, who try to discredit me: who try to bring me down, tell lies and are trying to get me out of my seat, but that's life, that's just another fight in my life which I intend to win. My drive stems from the fact that I care so much about others; my family, my friends, my constituency and the young people within it.

There will be lots of people in life who will not believe in you or your passion. Not everyone believed in me, but my family and friends' belief and support, and my own belief in myself is what kept me going.

When I became MP for Brent, those who originally tried to discourage me, actually apologised and said, "Dawn you're doing a great job, keep it up". Even more encouraging was Obama, who told me to, "Never stop achieving," and that he too was proud of me.

My advice to you would be don't set your targets low, as there will be enough people doing that for you. Set them high. Set them beyond even your own imagination.

Racism Amongst MP's

Parliament can still be a lonely and racist place. I remember using the members lift, and a few politicians started talking about how, "Cleaners and catering staff should not be allowed to use that lift", referring to me. I objected to the tone and content of the conversation, and informed the members that it was wrong to talk about people like that. I did not highlight the fact that I was an MP because that was not the point.

Making History

One of my greatest achievements as MP was becoming one of only three black female MP's ever, and the first African-Caribbean MP to become a minister. I can walk with my head held high because I worked extremely hard for it.

I campaign hard on issues which affect the ordinary person; poverty, unemployment, crime, health and my main area youth and youth services. I want to listen to what young people want and act as a voice for them.

The Power Of Oneself

One of my most favourite lines is from a song, sung by Robert Nester Marley, "Emancipate yourself from mental slavery, none but ourselves can free our minds".

This power of oneself is the most powerful force of change that there can ever really be. Think about it!!!

Michael Fuller

Who would have thought that I was actually going to
become what I said I would?' Most young people
change their minds a hundred times but I always
wanted to be a police officer.
Today I stand proud and receive my title of
the first black Chief Constable in Britain.

stand here proud of my achievements and look back
not with regret, but look to help those who want
to progress through the ranks.
I've worked hard and paved the way so that you can
believe and see that anything is possible.

did not come from a rich family, but I am now helping
oken families and stabilising communities. The saying
that your past does not determine your future is
something I believe in 100%

Athletics vs. Metropolitan Police

I was born in London but I grew up and went to school in Sussex. At school I was very well behaved and was very interested in sports.

My interest for sport kept me out of trouble and kept me focused and disciplined. I ran for my school a few times and won the County Schools 800m athletics championships.

I spent most of my time training at my athletics club, and had friends who were interested in sports just like me. We were driven by competition, and some of them actually went on to compete for England later on.

I was more interested in catching criminals and helping victims, so I focused more on becoming a police officer. When I was 16 ½ years old, I went to London to join the Metropolitan police on a two-year cadet scheme, which I really enjoyed.

Life As An Officer

I then won an ex-cadet scholarship to study Social Psychology at Sussex University. Then in 1977 I joined the Metropolitan Police. I was given my badge and my boots and became a trainee probationary officer in Fulham. There were only five other black officers in the force at this time, so it was very easy to spot me - now there's over 2,000 ethnic minority officers.

Did I get funny looks from my own people? Of course I did. I was called "traitor", "informer", "snitch" all sorts of things but I didn't care because I wanted to make the community a safer place to live in. I got mixed reactions because there were some black people encouraging me and telling me they were happy to see a black officer for a change, which pleased me.

Over the years I have arrested many criminals and some people would ask "Were you not scared?" No, I wasn't. I couldn't be. I had to go out there brave and confident otherwise I would have been putting my life in danger if I was afraid.

I remember soon after joining the Met Police that I surprised a burglar at the back of some shops and we got into a violent struggle. He attempted to stab me, but my back-up came just in time and he got arrested.

When you join the force they put you through a lot of training, where you're taught how to handle certain situations, including having a gun pointed at you or a knife held against you. No one will be let out onto the street if they don't pass their training or their fitness levels are unsatisfactory.

Criminals And Police Officers

Every day on the street was different for me. Every day I heard a new lie. I used to think to myself, "Do they actually think I'm going to believe that story?" Most criminals always think that they will never get caught. So when they eventually get busted a lot of them are shocked because they thought they could beat the law.

Working for the Met was great but when I first joined I did experience some racism. I had to learn very quickly that some people will like you and others won't. However I did not put up with the racism and I was vocal with my views on equality and fairness. Officers knew not to be racist towards criminals when we were out because I wasn't going to turn a blind eye.

Even when it came down to selecting officers, the procedure for selection improved; we had more women officers join the Met.

My passion for crime investigation led to me leading Operation Trident; one of the biggest initiatives to stop black on black gun crime within London urban areas. The message at the time was that no one was interested; even the media had stopped reporting the murders of black people because there were so many. So, I had to increase the awareness of this issue by getting communities to take more responsibility and be willing to become witnesses.

Catching Criminals

I also led more operations such as Operation Bumblebee and Operation Eagle Eye, which were very successful.
Operation Bumblebee was a burglary control program and Operation Eagle Eye was a strategy put in place to reduce the number of street robberies.

Whilst at Scotland Yard I was also involved in setting up the Racial and Violent Crime Task Force in response to the criticisms from the Stephen Lawrence inquiry about racism within the police force.

Unstoppable

So you can see I worked very hard, but I didn't always get promoted. I had to stay focused and determined. I was very ambitious and decided to do some private studying. I went on to do a Masters in Business Administration, post graduate diplomas in Law, Criminology and Marketing, and became a qualified barrister in 2007. Now with all of those qualifications under my belt, I had all the knowledge, the skills, the certificates and the hands on experience, I was unstoppable. I could have been happy with just being a constable or community police officer but I wanted to get to the top; be the one calling the shots, and I knew I was not going to get there by how many arrests I had made over the years. I made sure I was in a position to compete.

Now don't get me wrong, there are no specific qualifications for becoming a police officer but completing outside studying builds you up as an individual, it gives you more confidence and understanding but most of all it shows that you are willing to learn and develop.

You need to believe that you are just as good as the next man or woman. Don't ever be intimidated by another officer because of their rank. You should respect them but don't allow them to push you around. Even if you get knocked back, pick yourself up and try again.

Challenges
If you can't handle rejection then you will find life very difficult. There is no challenge or rejection that can't be overcome. Life will sometimes present itself as unfair but it should not be enough to deter you and make you into a quitter. Keep your eyes on the prize, and find other ways of overcoming barriers. I see failures as merely a setback and a challenge to be overcome.

There were times when I did not get my promotion but I did not allow that to deter me. I felt that I had to work twice as hard but it was worth it. You won't always be successful first time round but if you remain determined and positive then you will achieve success.

Genuine Passion
Joining the police force was a decision I made because of my passion to help communities, it was not because of the money. My life was at risk every day when I was out on the street but it was my passion that kept me going.

You wouldn't join the police force just for money as this job can never pay enough for one to risk their life. I'm still here after all these years because this is what I live for; helping others.

To survive in this job, you need to have lots of good common sense, you need to be calm, level headed, able to work in a team and able to use your own initiative when in an emergency. You also need to be motivated to help others and enjoy catching criminals. It has to be a job you love otherwise you won't last very long.

Focus, persistence, having self worth and knowing where you're going were all the ingredients I had and the ones mentioned above. Now I am the first black Chief Constable for Kent Police in Britain, managing over 6,170 police officers and support staff.

Freedom From Poverty
A lot of young people don't want to hear this but in order to get out of poverty you will have to work hard, whether it's for yourself or for somebody else. Sitting at home or hanging around on the streets is not really going to make you rich.

Studying is another route out of poverty. Even in downtown Kingston Jamaica the police officers said, "Education was the best route out of poverty". This surprised me as I thought the police officers were going to say, "We need more police on the streets" but they said, "It was education that was the greater need".

My Real Motivation

In 2004 the Queen awarded me a medal for my dedication and hard work to the Police Service but the most important recognition for me was from the communities and families I had helped over the years and from the young kids who would say, 'I want to be just like you when I'm older'.

I knew from when I was young that this was all I wanted to do. If I could improve the lives of just one family or a young person, or influence the laws of the land then I would be happy and I certainly have done all of those things.

People Can Change

Anything in this life is possible, you just have to believe. I recently bumped into the burglar that I surprised over ten years ago and he told me that he was now a changed man; a mentor to young offenders.

I was so surprised because he had quite a record from a young age, but it made me realise that people can change if simply given the right guidance and direction. They can then go on to become great role models to others just like them!

no more

eXcuses

Junior Phipps

"Teachers never made me feel like I was worth anything at school, and people never really showed interest in me, so it was up to me to make something of myself. I had to big myself up and motivate myself otherwise I would have become a rebel. I used all the negative things people would say to me to motivate me to keep going. No way was I going to prove anyone right, I knew I had the potential to be great even if no one else saw it in me.

Now I can say that I am one of the few black men who have had their own product featured on one of the most watched shows on TV; the Apprentice. Who would have thought a black man who grew up on one of the dirtiest and poorest council estates would be one of the most successful designers in 3D design and furniture making in England today? I did"

Dumping Ground

Dumping Ground

Growing up in Battersea was an experience. We lived in council flats for a long time and only moved to Streatham because they were knocking down the flats. Battersea was very notorious for being a dumping ground for council tenants, so it wasn't a nice area at all.

Even when we moved into our house in Streatham I shared a room with my brother, as the house was still not big enough for us to live comfortably.

My parents worked hard and supported me as much as they could in whatever I wanted to do but they were also very strict with me.
I thought I was right and they were wrong, but of course I had to do what they said. Back chatting Caribbean parents was not cool, it meant a well deserved beating.

Role Models

Some of my friends did not have both parents around but I realised that it was possible for them to still find role models outside of their immediate family. Not having a father around does not affect your life, but not having any role models can affect you. My dad was around all of the time but I was also drawing influence and wisdom from my uncles and friends fathers.

If your father is absent you can't focus on that for the rest of your life and become a failure, NO you go out and look for someone who can mentor you.

At school I was in the middle sets. I was lucky to have a black teacher called Mr. Hull. He would travel from Leeds to London everyday to teach us. He was one of the first people in my life who told me that I was clever, and all I had to do to move up in the sets was to try harder, to shine more in class, rather than just blending in.

I actually listened to him and I was moved up. I started to believe that I could actually achieve more in life. It meant a lot that he was able to see my potential and wanted me to do well. He got my respect from then on however some of the other teachers got my rude boy side, because of their prejudiced attitude against me, which resulted in me getting kicked out of sixth form.

Expelled

I got 4 GCSE's, which was all I needed to get into sixth form. I remember being in the assembly and they were calling up all the students to congratulate them for passing their GCSE's. Out of 200 students I was the last to be called. When it came to my turn, they blatantly said to me, "We don't want to take you on but you got the grades, so we have to". It actually made me happier that they hated the fact I had made it but later on I allowed them to get to me.

At sixth form, I fell out with a lot of my teachers and I finally got expelled. They told me that I was going to become nothing and that made me very 'MAD'. I wanted to prove them all wrong, to wipe the smug looks of their faces. So I decided to go and get some careers advice to find out what I could do next. I wasn't about to become a statistic; another black boy who had failed.

I applied to go to another college in Whitechapel, so everyday I had to travel from South London to East London to study. I wasn't sure of what area of design I wanted to go into so I did a BTEC National Diploma in Design, which allowed me to experience the many different areas I could go into.

By this time I was focused and knew that I was great at art and design. I showed my teachers my portfolio and they were very impressed. My portfolio contained life drawings, observational drawings and graphic designs. It was a reflection of how I thought of life and how I saw things.

I was very interested in design and went on to do a degree in 3D design. I then got a grant to do my Masters degree in Furniture Design & Technology, so I guess I was doing very well.

Failure Not An Option
My degree was not easy but it was my only option. If I didn't complete university then I would have had to make money other ways and it would have been the wrong way, so failure was not even an option for me and that's how I got through university.

I just worked hard and decided to give it my all. It did not enter my head to fail. I had a lot of deaths and illnesses around me at the time I was studying but I drew on that pain to succeed.

A degree is important as it helps you get to that level and learn the basics in design. It helps you to get grounded and gives you that extra knowledge. It also offers you that year to do work experience which will really help you to make contacts. A degree is not the only way forward but if I was to employ someone I would be looking for someone with a keen interest in design, knowledge of how to use the equipment with knowledge of health and safety.

Work Experience
You can do work experience in printing companies and graphic design companies. Approach successful designers and do volunteer work with them, where you're gaining more knowledge and skills in different trades. After that they may employ you as a junior designer, and teach you how to use certain software packages. They may even send you on a few training courses.

After doing my masters, I got my first job as a general technician at the college I went to. It was not a high paid job but it did help me pay the rent. The wages were actually an insult as I was way overqualified for the job. I had a Masters in design, so of course I was a bit frustrated.

The reason why I stayed on was due to the experience I was getting and the understanding of how to run a craft workshop. I learnt that you had to 'kiss ass' before you could 'kick ass', as my mum always said, so I did that for a year and then I applied for a teaching position.

I sent out fifty letters to colleges, had rejections from forty-nine colleges and only one replied, saying 'I can give you one day a week, three hours in the morning and three hours in the afternoon', I was so happy.
I used to look at my teachers and think, "If you're such a successful designer, why are you here?" They used to say, "You have good times and bad times, times when you're designing all day and other times when you will be doing nothing, so you have to keep yourself occupied".

I am now an associate lecturer at Camberwell University of the Arts, London. I teach BA (Hons) 3D design there and I'm a 3D design specialist lecturer at Richmond upon Thames College. I decided that the teaching route would be good for me, as I was doing something that was still within the same creative field and bringing in money during the dry seasons.

Conscious Forms
One of the high points of my career was when I was chosen out of twenty designers to be on the second series of the 'Apprentice'. The contestants had to try and sell my product to different shops, which was very exciting.
Some of my other products have been featured on the BBC2 Lifestyle Home Show and on ITV's 60 Minute Makeover.

My signature product, the one people mainly know me for is the concrete lighting product Lite3, which is a sculptural low voltage halogen lamp in a formed concrete cube. They are sold in retail shops and galleries who sell design or craft based products.

Being self employed means that you have to do a lot of the marketing yourself, which is the hardest part of it for me. I have to do exhibitions all the time, so I fly out to Milan yearly.

Milan is the trade show of the year for furniture and product design, as it's in Europe, in-between the middle of the Far East and America. It costs around £4,000 all inclusive to have a stand there, but you can get funding for it.

My company, which I set up in 2005, is called 'Conscious Forms'. I believe in putting positive messages onto products. This year I designed 'The Gandhi Mirror', which has inspiring reflective quotes engraved on the surface like '...You must be the change you wish to see in this world'. I love illusion; creating different perceptions using multi-faceted textures to bring a consciousness into my products.

Branching Out

Furniture design is not an area that many black people go into. We do design some of our own cultural furniture but we need to branch out; cater for all types of people and environments. When I go out to Milan, there are over 300 stands there, but only 3 out of the 300 stands belong to black business owners. I feel proud to be there because it means I'm able to compete with other successful designers.

I've learnt not to get angry, but to get intellectual on people who try to look down on me for being black. In this field of work, skin colour can be irrelevant; it's all about your product. Let your work sing for you and then step out into the lime light.

With a degree in 3D furniture design, you can work in an industrial company designing trains, planes, products and cars, or you can work for a creative theatre company designing TV sets and back drops. You can even go into interior design or architecture, which may require a bit more of studying, so you can transfer your skills.

Recognition

I've won a few awards; a Design and Innovation award with CEN magazine, which stands for Creative Enterprise Networks which was really good. I also won two awards through Hidden Art, an agency that supports designers and another award for Up and Coming Designers.

To be able to make it in this design industry you have to persevere, have belief in yourself and let your creativity shine.

Becky Eleazu

" My eagerness and curiosity led to me becoming
egnant at the age of seventeen. Everyone told me that I
as too young to have a baby and that my life was over.

ow at the age of thirty six years old I can look back and
ay to all the critics, doubters and gossipers that I am a
oud mother of three, an entrepreneur, and a role model
to my children and their friends "

The Pressures

I was born In Chelsea to Nigerian parents. We lived in a nice house with a fantastic family atmosphere. My parents worked very hard and were great role models to me as they always persevered no matter what.

You would think coming from a nice area and a good home I would have behaved myself, but that was not the case. I was a bit rebellious for a 'Nigerian girl' as I wanted to go out and have boyfriends, so I would sneak behind my mums back.

I was too hard of hearing and wanted to be my own boss. At the time my mum was like 'Dennis the Menace'; so annoying, but really all she was trying to do was protect me.

Being a bright kid, I got a few B's and C's for my GCSE's but of course my parents said, "You could have done better". My mum always said to me, "If another child got a B, then you must get an A." Really, she meant that as a Nigerian you must always be at the top of the class.

Unexpected Reactions

I decided to study Media at college because my older brother had made a success of himself through presenting children's BBC. I thought it looked like fun.

However at the age of seventeen, I became pregnant. I thought my mum would be disappointed with me and see me as a let down but she was the opposite and became my rock and my best friend.
However she was not going to allow me to become another statistic, so I was off to college that year to complete what I had started.

Many people tried to tell me that I would not make it, that my life was ruined and I was going to live in a council flat for the rest of my life.
Never once did my mum turn her back on me, it was her strength that made me believe I could do it.

Determined

I went on to study Fashion and Retail Management at London College of Fashion and I was in four times a week. I had to live off £53.00 a week with a child to clothe and feed but I was determined to succeed. I knew if I could only imagine the future I wanted, then I could make it happen.

There were times when my mum was working and I had coursework deadlines, so I had to sneak my baby into the library and hide her under the table. I didn't feel ashamed, as I was not about to fail university and go back to living off £53.00 a week.

I didn't wait for any hand outs but took control of my life and made it happen with the support of my mother. Remember that babies soon grow up and you struggle less, so just hold on.

I remember saying to my mum, "I want to be a window dresser". She couldn't understand why I wanted to dress a window. I then decided to be a buyer as I saw that that was where the real money was.

The Reality

When I finished university I couldn't get the job I wanted as I had no selling experience. I was told to do two years of selling on the shop floor before I could get the actual job I was qualified for.

This was hard for me to take but I didn't give up and for two years I did what I had to do. I then went on to get a buying job for a company called Sage, buying designer labels for them to sell in their shop. I worked for them for seven years, getting the experience and knowledge. They told me that anything was possible and they led me to believe that I could have what they had.

I used to go to fashion shows and fill my glass up with water as I couldn't afford to buy champagne. I understood that I needed to be around the right kind of people, those who could teach me.

Starting My Own Business

When I decided to leave Sage, I left to start up my own business. I had a beautiful open shop in Clapham, which was doing very well until the market closed down. I was selling all sorts of designer clothes which were the real deal, but every night I had to pack up the clothes and put them out again the next day, what I needed was a real shop.

So my partner and I went to look for shops to rent and we found the perfect place. It was a derelict building that had been dormant for seven years because the owner did not want to rent it out. However, I believed that it was mine.

So I went to the shop and spoke to the man. He didn't want to rent it out but he said to me, "There's something about you Becky that I like, it's yours".

If I never believed and chased my dream then I would never have gotten that shop. I believed in what I was doing and what I could do.

I knew fashion and I knew how to style people. I also knew how to go out and cherry pick the best designer clothes out there to sell in my boutique, so the customers wouldn't have to go elsewhere.

'Balham Bou Exposed'

Starting up my beautiful boutique was tough. I did not have financial support, everything that went into the shop; time, work and money all came from mine and my partner's pockets.

We needed £50,000 to start up the boutique and to do it up, and that was all our savings.

I would say, "Don't take the risk, if you're not willing to follow through on your dream, because you will give up too easily".

We turned the derelict building into a beautiful designer shop called 'Rumpelstiltskin'. It was my partner, my daughter and I who did the painting, put up the lights and built the changing rooms. It was purely a D.I.Y job as we could not afford to pay anyone. I got a book and found out how to put up false walls. I built my office, the fixtures and fittings in the shop; everything. If there's not enough money you will have to improvise.

There were times when the shop was doing well and times when it wasn't. It was at this point that Max my partner suggested we go on 'Mary, Queen of Shops'. I thought he was mad. He wanted me to go on national TV and declare to the world, that we were in debt by £10,000. I told him, "No way!" Now I'm so happy he talked me around.

From Debt To Riches

Within the first week of the show going on the TV, the takings tripled. The name of the shop changed to 'Balham Bou' and people were actually coming in. The show changed my life and my wallet size.

Mary Portas was a fantastic role model to me. She is the best in her field and she mentored me. I am now even more successful. The boutique caters for Balham's young professionals and stocks popular brands like FCUK and Mina UK.

Surprise!

I remember when I used to talk on the phone and book meetings with the receptionists of different designers. I would give them my name and they would say, "We can't wait to see you". I would then arrive at the building, press the buzzer and say, "Its Becky" and they would let me up. Having arrived at the desk, they would ask, "Who are you?" I would then say, "I'm Becky" and they would be like, "Really?" They were so shocked to see a beautiful black girl speaking so well and doing so well.

Success!

Being black does not make you second best. I'm just as intelligent as another person of any other race. The fact that some young people can run successful illegal enterprises means that they have the skill, discipline and determination of a legit business man.

They know how to wake up on time and stay until the deal is done. So why not take all that knowledge and use it for something positive?

To run a successful boutique, you need to immerse yourself within the whole fashion industry, know what's on trend, and go to all the fashion events.

Preparation really is the key: failure to prepare is definitely preparing to fail. You first need to gain some knowledge by working for someone else. Selling clothes really isn't easy. When they said I needed experience I thought they were taking the mick, but I realised that not everyone has the gift of selling or knows how to work the shop floor naturally.

My customers like the fact that I am honest with them and also friendly. They trust my advice and styling. They know that I will never allow anyone to walk out of Balham Bou unless they're looking fabulous.

Having the qualifications and experience is what you will need as a black person to make it big in this industry as there will be a lot of hurdles to jump over, but with those things under your belt, no one can tell you NO.

A Woman of Many Talents

I now do styling for a lot of music videos with a video production company called Digital Holdings. I styled Sheya for the song 'Dream Come True' which came to No.6 in the MTV Base charts. I also do consultancy and personal image styling. I've styled models for London Fashion Week, programs for Channel 4 and for a video called 'Rolling with the Nine's'.

My Support Network

My partner of twenty years stuck by me and supported me, my mum was a pillar to me and my children were an inspiration to me. Without that support and mentorship from others my dream would have been much harder to fulfill but I still would have made it, because I'm not a quitter.

Aml Ameen

Jhen people see me in my local shops they ask me for
J autograph, congratulate me and then ask me what I'm
oing in an ordinary shop. Yes I have been in a few films
•nd been nominated for a BAFTA, but behind all of that I
really am a normal guy with a big dream.

ome people see me as a role model; an inspiration, and
at makes me smile, but what's more important to me is
hat I don't stop achieving. I want to be the best I can be
d will make all the sacrifices I have to just to get to that
oint. Others put 100% into their work but I put in 110%
because I don't want to leave any room for excuses

Barbara Speake Stage School

I was born in North West London in 1985, but spent most of my youth in West London where I went to stage school. I remember saying to my parents that I wanted to be an actor after watching Home Alone. My parents believed in my dream and took me to one of the best stage schools around; Barbara Speake Stage School.

Growing up was very different for me because I was exposed to a professional environment of television from the age of six. I was in '123 Hullabaloo' with Floella Benjamin, and at the age of eleven I was one of the kids on the stage at the 1996 Brit Awards singing the earth song with Michael Jackson. I was acting in West End musicals such as 'Oliver Twist' and featured in 'Grange hill', so life was pretty busy for me.

I didn't have the time to hang on road or mess about in class because I had to succeed! I was in a very competitive environment, so being the best was not an option, it was the only option. I went to the same school as Damage, Ultimate Kaos, Naomi Campbell, Michelle Gayle and many more famous people, so I had the potential to do well if I remained focused and determined.

Supportive Parents

The fees for Barbara Speake Stage School were very expensive and I did not come from a wealthy background so I knew that my parents had to work very hard to keep me there. They did all that they could do to support me financially throughout my ten years at Stage School, in particular my dad

The Attitude Of An Actor

Growing up I couldn't be negative at all. Everyday I had to strive to be the best, even if I didn't get the part I wanted. At the age of fifteen I was told I had received a part in a drama written around the Stephen Lawrence story, however at the last minute the role was given to another actor. Of course I was devastated but I realised that this was the reality in my industry.

Experiences like this strengthened me and taught me the importance of being excellent with every opportunity I got.

Growing up, the TV shows I loved watching were 'Fresh Prince of Bel-Air', 'Sister Sister', and 'Kenan and Kel'. I drew a lot of inspiration from them but now Denzel Washington is a great role model to me. I respect everything he represents as a black man and I love his films

Barnet College

I completed stage school at the age of sixteen and went to Barnet College to study drama and film studies.

This was a big culture shock for me as I grew up in a predominantly white school.

Barnet College had such a big cultural mix and had a very urban, youthful environment; the energy was explosive. I enjoyed my time there and made some really good friends.

Little did I know that I was soon to play leading roles in films of characters that were just like those around me.

Kidulthood - The Leading Man

I auditioned for Kidulthood in 2003 for the part of Trife, the film's leading man, and I got it. However when the film collapsed I had to re-audition in 2004 and didn't get the part immediately (like all the other members of the cast). I think this was because I didn't come with the right focus needed; I had become a bit too comfortable. When I got the call for my third and final audition, I was driven by the previous rejection and I wanted the part desperately.

I went home and learnt the whole script. At the audition I recited the part where Trife tells his girlfriend that he loves her, one of the final most emotionally demanding scenes in the film. I performed that scene three times with three different actresses; tears, kisses, everything. Each time I finished the scene, I would turn and look at the director (Menhaj Huda) in his eyes; it was then that he knew I was ready, and the best man for the job.

I honestly believe that this experience was one of the most defining moments for me as an actor. From that day forward, I realised the importance of being prepared with my work, and having the passion and dedication needed to create that magic which enables others to believe in you.

The Bill - Police Officer Lewis Hardy

A year later in 2005, I got the part of the now legendary character, police officer Lewis Hardy in the Bill. I was nineteen years old when I got this part and it was amazing. As Lewis I got to be everything; the action hero and the rebel, and I also got to act out a few romantic scenes which made Lewis into a heart throb.

So in January 2006 my episodes in the Bill were shown on TV and Kidulthood came out in the cinemas March 2006. This was an exciting time for me career wise as people now knew me as an actor; they knew me by my real name and not by the names of the characters I played.

My final episodes in the Bill, 'Salvation', were also nominated for a BAFTA award. I was the only black person in The Bill and my scene was up on the large screen; I felt good. I won a Best Actor award at the 'Screen Nation Awards 2007'.

Another special moment for me was when I attended a Choice FM event "Junior Jam" as a guest. The host Pheobe1 called me on stage and the crowd erupted, that was definitely one of my first career highlights, I didn't expect that reaction!

The WOW Factor

Acting is not just about acting, it's about making the whole character come to life; taking your audience on a journey where they believe in the world you have created and they feel your emotions.

A really good movie and a great performance can affect lives, I have seen it; people, especially the youth have been so involved in some of my work it's phenomenal.

Actors Student Alliance

I have now started up my very own acting company called ASA (Actors Student Alliance), where I have thirty aspiring actors from the ages of 16 – 38 and I teach them everything I know, from adopting the right attitude as an actor, to being punctual which is very important. I also teach them drama techniques, how to break down characters, theatrical acting and script writing.

The commitment and punctuality of an actor is tough. My daily routine whilst I was shooting The Bill was - up for 5.00am, leave my house at 6.00am, get to work for 7.30am and be on set for 8.00am on the dot. I would then be filming for the whole day and get back home for 9.00pm. This was a long day for me but I didn't mind because I was willing to work hard to achieve my goals and get that continued success.

Also I love what I do; the acting, the filming, the whole thing. In the Bill I was allowed to be creative with my character which made playing Lewis Hardy, a young urban cop even more interesting.

Fallout - Dwayne The Murderer

One of the most challenging characters I have ever had to play was Dwayne in the TV film Fallout in 2008, which was shown on Channel 4. The film written by Roy Williams was inspired by the tragic murders of both Damilola Taylor and Stephen Lawrence. In this film, I played a cold, calculated gang leader who murdered a young black boy.

Playing the character of a villain was different for me and quite a stretch from my own personality.

I had to work really hard just so I could get into the mind of a person like Dwayne and make him become real to the audience, taking them on a journey.

Do You Have What It Takes?

I usually say to my ASA class, "In life you have the winners and the onlookers; you have to decide which one you're going to be. This industry is not for everyone as it can be a very up and down journey, so do you honestly have what it takes?"

As a test to my students I make them face each other, run on the spot at full speed, screaming their dreams at the top of their lungs. The first person to give up means they are not passionate enough about their dream. This game is not about fitness, but about your hunger to succeed.

There was a time in my class when two boys were facing each other and they were running on the spot for a long time. They started to take off their jumpers, their hats, all sorts because they didn't want to loose and in the end they ended up motivating each other to go further and they both won. It was amazing to see.

Pushing forward when you feel like quitting is the true testament of character. I will never quit because I love that feeling of achievement.

Do You Have A Dream?

As a young person, I feel that it is so important for other young people to have a sense of purpose in their life. It's important to know that whatever your goal is in life, it can be and is meant to be achieved, so take inspired actions towards it.

I had a dream at the age of six to be a Hollywood movie star and now I am one of the leading young actors in the UK; my journey is not complete but I'm on my way. It's not easy and you make your everyday sacrifices but you have your blessings also.

Aspiring Actors

If you want to become an actor then drama workshops are a good place to begin and drama school if you can afford it. Find yourself an agent and get work through them. There are so many avenues to take, but you just have to find the right one for you.

Aml Ameen'

I have a saying that has motivated me since I was sixteen, "Art is man's signature on time," and that pretty much sums up my ambitions with my career. When I'm long gone I want to be sure that my name will shine in the history books.

no more

eXcuses

Trevor Robinson

> t many people believed in what I wanted to do as they
> ad never seen it done before in the U.K. I didn't need to
> see it work; I believed it could be done. Even when my
> business partner and producer left me, I still remained
> cused and determined, and look at me now! One of the
> ost memorable Heat adverts ever made was produced
> by my company; Quiet Storm

My Childhood

I grew up in a loving household with my three brothers and a sister. We were a working class family. My dad was a self made businessman who had a painting and decorating company. Mum was a cook by day and by night she was a cleaner, always working hard to pay the bills.

I was fortunate to live in a house that my dad bought however things weren't as good as they seemed. By the age of nine my parents split up and we lost the house. Life became very different as we moved into a flat in Clapham with my mum. The area was pretty rough and a lot of my friends were in and out of prison. It was a horrible estate to live in.

I used to get stopped and searched by the police but I never got into trouble. However if I never had any talents or dreams to pursue then there was a good chance that I may have been drawn into a different lifestyle eventually.

I knew that life wasn't going to be easy when my dad later on became an alcoholic. Before he got to that state he was my role model. He came to this country as a stranger, with no qualifications and was able to set up his own business and buy a house. It was because of him that I actually got into film. He would always take me out on a Sunday to watch cowboy films which I loved!

My Passion For Art

Whilst growing up I had a lot of people who made it their business to tell me that I wouldn't amount to much in life. At school I was advised by one of my tutors that I should become a bus conductor. At first it did affect me, but I knew I was going to be alright somehow, even though later on I did spend a period of my life on the dole after leaving college.

I used to bunk off from school and go to free exhibitions at South Bank and watch films in the cinema. My passion for art grew whilst I was at secondary school and by the third year, I was one of the top students in my art class.

However I wasn't as strong in my other subjects. Sadly I didn't get all my O-Levels but I did have a decent art portfolio that got me into college. At the time I used to attend a lot of life classes and make a lot of comics to keep me occupied and learning.

Everything I drew went into my portfolio. I got into South Thames College because the teachers were really impressed with the amount of work I had done. They could see from my portfolio that I was really passionate about art.

The Real World

I left college early as I wanted to work in the creative industry right away.

(I wouldn't advise you to do that now but things were very different in the late 70s.) However I needed some income so I eventually got a part time job in Tesco's. It wasn't the best job, but I was happy because I was making more money than some of the others on my block who were doing illegal activities.

Working allowed me to go to more places and to do things related to where I was heading.

I didn't know 100% what my future looked like but I knew I wanted to work in the creative industry. People could see I wasn't moving anywhere fast and one day an old girlfriend turned to me and said, "Why don't you just go and work for my dad, why are you doing this?" She could not understand why I was putting myself through the stress of trying to get a job in a specific industry. As far as I was concerned, there was no other option; this was what I wanted to do.

Even with a part time job times were hard for me, and on a few occasions I ran out of money having to go for interviews and building up my portfolio.

I remember emptying out my money box a couple of times counting the very last pennies, but I still persevered and remained determined.

Starting At The Bottom

I wanted a job as an animator but a company that had shown interest in me blew me out, so I took an offer from a graphic design company instead. They seemed to be more interested in me being a tea maker and keeping me working for them as a junior. I thought, "Nah, let me aim higher". Eventually I ended up in advertising.

I started off at the bottom, working for Samuels & Pearce, an advertising agency but after a year I left because I felt like the life was being sucked out of me. I knew that if I really wanted to make it big, I had to go and work in the West End.

I stayed at S&P for so long because I was earning a bit of money and getting the experience I needed but I knew that life had to be better than this, so while working for S&P I continued to work on my portfolio.

When it hit evening time, I would meet up with my friend and we would work on our portfolios in his office till morning time and then go to work.

We kept on doing this until one day my boss at S&P called me into his office to tell me some great news.....

"You're Fired"

He said, "Trevor I'm going to sack you because I know that you want to leave, but I'm also going to give you some money to help you". So he fired me, however that was one of the best decisions ever made for me by someone else.

West End

It took me a year before I eventually broke into the West End. I got fired from one West End agency but managed to get into another one. It was at this agency that I produced the award winning Orange Tango advert - 'You know when you've been Tango'd' as well as a few other well recognised campaigns, but I wanted to move on to do my own thing.

Deserted And Alone

So in 1995, I left my job with my good friend to start up our own venture. However after a short while my partner returned back to our old agency because he was not 100% sure about the business. I also had a producer who joined the team but got cold feet and left, so I became a lone soldier with a dream.

I must have been really brave at the time because I was going to start up my very own company that had never been done in the UK before. I wanted to have the best of both worlds under one umbrella. I wanted to have an advertising agency that came up with creative ideas for clients and their brands and also a production company to produce the ads. I knew I was taking a risk, but I was willing to do it as I believed in myself.

Quiet Storm

Quiet Storm was founded in 1995 and I was able to find a committed team of people who believed in this new agency structure. Over the last thirteen years we have grown each year and our clients now include Kerry Foods, HMV, COI and Haribo.

The reason why we have grown is because of the results we have created for our clients. When we first started working on Heat magazine seven years ago it was about to close with sales of only 60,000 per week, since then we have created some of publishing's most successful advertising ever and turned Heat into a 600,000 weekly selling cultural icon and market leader.

The reaction I get from the viewers after my advert goes on TV is electric. No one knows who I am but when my advert comes on in the cinema people burst out laughing, or say, "That's serious!" That's what keeps me going, the fact that people can still remember my adverts a year down the line.

Never Give Up

To become successful you need to identify who you are, what you like to do, where you would like to take it, and then go for it 100%. You need to put yourself out there by networking with the relevant people, showing them your portfolio.

Don't be afraid of rejection because it does come, sometimes too often, but you just have to rise above it and keep going. I've known a lot of talented people who have stopped believing and just given up. I could have given up on my dreams a long time ago and worked for someone else, but I knew I would have been living a life of regret. I had already made too many sacrifices to get to where I wanted to be; I wasn't looking to stop half way.

I remember when I used to go out to exhibitions or go to the cinema and people on the council estate used to ask me, "Why are you leaving the block?" When I told them I was going to the West End, they would then say, "What, you think you're posh or something?"

I wanted to experience the whole world, so I was ready to leave my friends. I had a future I needed to make happen. A lot of my friends had potential but no one aimed high enough, their lives were centred on the block. I know if I ever went back today, those same boys now men would probably still be there.

Pursuing My Goals

Everyday I jump out of my bed, excited because I have a great company to go to. Gone are the days of scrounging for money and working my backside off for others.

A few years ago I was always one step away from tripping up and going back to living off the dole, now I can say I'm far away from that place and every day I move further away as I continue to pursue my goals.

no more

eXcuses

Brenda Emanus

Working for the BBC has been both a rewarding and challenging experience. It certainly has not been an easy route to becoming a correspondent. I have throughout my career had my attacks of insecurity; wondering if I could do the job, or still had a job, but the competitiveness of the industry makes this all part of the process.

Everyone goes through it no matter how confident they may appear. Many people have joined the corporation and left, yet I am proud to say that after twenty years, seven of which have been spent in this job – I am still here!

I used to always feel the pressure of having to look good and appear slim and attractive but I don't pay as much attention to that anymore. I hate the idea of all presenters looking the same and believe strongly that television needs to show variety and be reflective of the audiences that it serves.

I'm not going to be any lighter skinned, any slimmer or wear shorter skirts just to appeal to certain people. I feel that integrity is important in my job so I won't bow to sexism or tolerate racism

Peer Pressure vs. Education

I was born in Camberwell, South London. My parents are from St.Lucia and are traditional West Indians; loyal, hardworking Christians with high moral values and huge ambitions for their children. They were surprisingly quite open minded about people, yet strict with us in terms of allowing us to go out. Work and school came before parties and raving everytime.

Education was extremely important to my family. I remember my mum sitting with me as a child and making me recite, "c-a-t, cat, r-a-t, rat, d-o-g, dog," before I even started going to school. I also remember her teaching me how to hold a pen the correct way and write. My parents saw education as my passport to freedom - not boys, not friends. I didn't mind because I actually loved school.

My Fake Jamaican Accent

There were times when I wanted to fit in at school with the cool and confident girls, so I would mess about and act up in class just so I could fit in. There were times my friends would say to me, "You think you're white!" just because I was in the top sets and classes.

I used to walk around school trying to speak in a Jamaican dialect even though my parents were not Jamaican just to fit in but my mum was having none of it and was always on my case.

I wanted to be part of a group, but not at the expense of failing my exams. I didn't want to let my parents, my teachers, or myself down. I remember my friends used to laugh at me for always studying, while they were out with boys.

My teachers used to become frustrated when they would see me messing around and would always remind me of my full potential and all that I could be. I was fortunate that they recognised my potential and invested time in to me- all that I had to do was focus and do well.

Making Up My Mind

At college I had no idea of what I really wanted to do as a career, so I chose subjects that I was simply interested in. I thought I was going to be an actress at one point but I soon realised once I went to youth drama school that there would be limited parts for me as a black woman at the time.

I've always loved travel and it was once suggested to me by my careers teacher that I join the army but the thought of having to wear uniform did not appeal to me. It was at that point that I discovered a Media Studies degree so I went off to study that at what is now known as Westminster University.

It was a big deal for me to go to University as not many of my friends did. It was exciting and scary all at once. I developed my independence and started to get a sense of a work environment as everyone had to sell themselves while learning to work together, be creative and compete.

Self Esteem Issues

My mother had always instilled in me that as a black woman I would have to work 'twice as hard' and I took that on board but on an even deeper level. I misinterpreted that to mean that I had to work harder because I was not good enough.

My lack of self confidence has always been an issue for me but it was balanced out by the fact that I always had really supportive people around me fuelling the fact that I was worth something.

Rejection And Opportunity

There were times when I would get rejected for jobs and quite naturally I would question whether my 'race' had anything to do with it, but I've learnt that the best thing to do is not to get bitter but to get better. I believe strongly that your talent and experience should stand for a lot and I don't allow such rejections to eat me up. If something is meant for me then it will be. I made a decision in my career that it was important for me to create my own networks and opportunities, simply by keeping my eye on the prize and remaining focused.

I remember interviewing the editor of the 'Voice' newspaper for my university project and by the end of the interview he had offered me a job. He said he liked my interviewing style and personality and so when I finished my degree, having freelanced for them in my spare time, I got a job as a news journalist.

Career Path

I then specialised in Arts and Entertainment and became the arts editor for the 'Voice', wrote music articles for 'Black Beat International' and then worked on the women's magazine 'Chic,' which has now evolved into 'Pride' magazine.

I then left the 'Voice' newspaper to join the BBC. It was the first job that I had applied for at the BBC, as a researcher on the talk show 'Kilroy.' My role involved getting in suitable audience members depending on the subject matter, and writing briefs for the presenter Robert Kilroy Silk. I briefed guests and then found suitable subjects to make programmes about.

While working there I also worked for BBC Breakfast Time as a researcher and then assistant producer. I thought I would end up being a producer long term as becoming a presenter had not been a part of my game plan.

I then left to become the arts and entertainment Reporter for Channel 4 News. This is when I discovered what I was really passionate about. I loved theatre, entertainment, fashion, music, drama, travel - all that area, so this job suited me perfectly.

Pick Yourself Up And Try Again

My big break after Channel 4 News was when I joined BBC 1 'The Clothes Show.' I became one of the main presenters and remained there for over five years. This was one of my highest profile jobs that definitely changed my life and fortunes. I thoroughly enjoyed traveling the world interviewing designers and shooting fashion stories.

Although it was one of my greatest times it also proved to be one of my toughest experiences, when I was informed that they wanted to replace me with someone that would have more appeal to mainstream younger girls.

I had to pick myself up and my ego and get on with it quite quickly; I couldn't be down for too long because I understood the way the media industry worked.

I soon got another job as the host of BBC's Midweek National Lottery and then worked as a freelance fashion and entertainment expert for Richard Madeley and Judy Finnigan on 'This Morning.' At the same time I presented some features for the BBC's 'Holiday' programme, and a health and travel programme and money programme for the Sky channel.

BBC London News

I am now the Arts, Culture and Entertainment Correspondent for BBC London News. My brief includes once again anything to do with this genre- from gallery openings, film premieres, music and red carpet events. I get to interview celebrities, actors, singers, performers and all form of creatives. We have to ensure that our output on BBC London is reflective of London and its communities which is an exciting challenge.

Famous People I've Interviewed

I have been fortunate to interview so many great people over the years. From Will Smith, Clint Eastwood and Stevie Wonder to Tracey Emin, Russell Simmons and Celine Dion. I've even met Muhammad Ali which was one of the highlights of my career.

My reporting style is pretty relaxed and informal. I love my job which is why I am still here. There have been many times when I've had really hard days at work, but it is my passion for the job and my commitment to do my best that keeps me going.

I realise how fortunate I am but I have had to work hard for this. I get extremely positive feedback from both mainstream and minority communities and that really encourages me.

The Reality Of The Media

As a journalist I was fuelled by my hunger for knowledge. I loved learning about things. I enjoyed writing and my natural curiosity became an advantage in my work. You do have to develop thick skin in this line of work because you are not going to be pleasing to everyone and the sooner you accept that the better.

The exciting thing about the media is how much it is changing and the widening opportunities that are available to people. Never forget that it is also a hugely competitive industry which can be backbiting and you have to learn to avoid the politics and focus on professionalism.

My advice to you is to build up a network of contacts as soon as you can because this is an arena that relies so much on contacts and who you know.

Awards

I believe your talent will speak for itself. I've won a few awards over the years, such as the Media Award from the Federation of Black Women Business Owners and the Voice Media Award to name a few.

I am also a visiting professor for the University of the Arts and a supporter of African Caribbean Leukemia Trust but my greatest achievement is that I am still working for the BBC after all these years.

Karl George

At a very young age I knew that my
future was going to be great!

was the kind of teenager who was always thinking of
ways to make money! Now at the age of 40, I am
recognised as one of the high profile 100 Certified
Accountants internationally, a very successful
entrepreneur, a great motivational speaker, a mentor to
many, a pastor, a husband and a proud father

The Early Years

I grew up in inner city Birmingham in the Perry Barr area under the care of my parents, brother and sister. At the age of seven I remember my grandma telling me that I was going to be an accountant because I was good at maths and I agreed with her. Knowing my grandma herself was a very successful business woman meant that one day I knew I would work hard to follow in her footsteps.

Despite having a very good relationship with my parents, when it came down to education there was no messing around; I was expected to do well. However by the age of thirteen I actually stopped enjoying school and never got serious about education again until I was twenty one. So for eight years, what was I doing?

1st Business

Well my first distraction and my first love was Karate. I used to attend Karate classes and ended up teaching them when my teacher turned up late, which was quite often. This inspired me and I realised that I could start up my very own Karate class and get paid for it. I was only fifteen years old at the time and I had about fifty young people in attendance.

2nd Business

Around the same time I also initiated a dance group called the 'Wild Flash Crew'. We danced across Birmingham; taking part in shows, entering competitions and winning them. We were pretty good!

3rd Business

At the age of seventeen, I started travelling to America, where I would buy all the latest styles and bring them back to England to sell to my friends. Even though my businesses were only small enterprises, I was able to learn good business principles from each of them, which later set me up for when I started my larger businesses.

Torn Between Education And Business

Even though I was doing very well with my small businesses, I never did fulfill my true potential at school. I managed to get satisfactory grades, but if I had worked harder, I know I could have gone to Oxford or Cambridge University. Instead of studying, I allowed my outside interests such as karate, dancing and chasing girls to get in the way of my education.

Even though I was a very talented and ambitious young man, I should have used my time more effectively to get the best out of my education and still have enough time to do the things I wanted to do.

Even whilst doing my A-Levels I still wasn't serious enough, and I ended up getting B, D and E grades. Due to this, I decided to go straight into work instead of going to university and did a foundation course in accountancy. I then got myself a job.

Studying and working at the same time took a lot of hard work and determination. It was at this point that I decided to give up my Karate classes in order to concentrate. Even though this was a big sacrifice for me, I knew that Karate was not my future; accountancy was, so it made sense.

Standing Out

The world of accountancy is very competitive. To find employment part time with an accountancy firm while studying for the ACCA qualification to become a qualified accountant can be very difficult, so it's important that you stand out when you go for an interview.

Doing extracurricular activities such as the Duke of Edinburgh Award, running a martial arts club, writing for a magazine or anything else that you enjoy will make the employers want to look at your CV.

The Only Black Person Not On The Shop Floor

I got my first job after working on a temporary contract for a month as a wage clerk at an engineering company called Brockhouse Transmission Limited. I always did more than was needed of me so that I would get recognised and promoted.

Unfortunately, while working there I did experience some discrimination in the early days. As the only black person not working on the shop floor, my boss did not like the fact that I had the potential to replace him one day. He always told me about jobs I should apply for outside of the company in order to get rid of me. I decided not to let him hold me down or to stop me from progressing.

He soon left and guess who got his job? Me! So, at the age of twenty three I was the youngest company accountant the company had ever had. I had a lot of responsibility as I was now managing the whole finance department for the company and as a young, black man, this was very rare.

I believe that my promotion was down to my willingness to stand out from the other accountants. I always took on extra roles at work and often stayed behind late which allowed me to build a good relationship with the managing director.

To become an average accountant all you need to have are the basic skills such as being analytical and having a good memory, but to become an excellent accountant you need to have transferable skills such as communication, presentation and interpersonal skills which are hard to find in this type of work. You need to show your boss or clients that you are self motivated and have very good self management skills.

4th Business: George Leedham

Even though I was good at my job, I was made redundant at Brockhouse. I looked for a job as a finance director but was told by other companies that I was too young. This gave me the drive to set up my own accountancy practice called George Leedham.

George Leedham was a very successful practice, employing around fifteen people and catering for clients with up to £20 million turnovers. After five years I decided to merge with an even bigger company called Andersons who had been running for seventy five years, we called ourselves Andersons KBS.

Merging was a big risk for me as it could have gone really well or I could have lost everything, but thank God it turned out to be a successful choice.

Going into partnership with someone just because you're friends is not a good idea; you need to be able to compliment each other with your skills. If you're good at accountancy find someone who is good at sales, so that you both have something to bring to the business.

As a business man, it's important to take calculated risk so you can grow to the next level. The bigger the risk, the more money you are able to make but you need to weigh up your options as you could either win or lose.

5th, 6th 7th, 8th business:

Even while I was the managing director for George Leedham, I had a number of other small businesses running. One of these was a recruitment agency for accountants. Recruitment was one of the fastest growing industries at the time.

I also started a sales business for golf membership, an events management company and a magazine business. I was very busy at this time but I knew how to manage my time effectively, which really helped.

9th Business: KgISS

In 2006 I sold my share in Andersons KBS and started up another company called KgISS. At KgISS, we work with the chief executives of companies to help them to work more effectively with their leadership, particularly in the area of governance. I sold my share as I felt that this was the perfect time to move on to another great business idea.

To become a great business man you need to be disciplined and organised. You also need to understand the nature of business, finance, sales, marketing, and networking. You need all of these tools and skills to make your business a success.

Studying business will give you an advantage over others who just have experience but you must bear in mind that you learn business by doing business. Do little trial businesses, little "runnings" we used to call it, to see how good you are and what areas you may need to improve on.

Role Models

My first role models when starting George Leedham were three black men from Birmingham; one was a property developer, another owned a glass manufacturing company and my third mentor had his own McDonalds franchise. It was good to see black men who had proper businesses that were doing very well.

Having a mentor is very important as they can help to speed up the process of you becoming successful. Even if you cannot meet them, you can look to what they have done and be inspired.

I have a passion not just for business but also to help those within my community. I established the 'first international chapter of 100 Black Men'; an organisation that encourages successful black men to mentor young black teenagers and help them to reach their goals.

Multi - Award Winning Business Man

I have a strong will to achieve all my goals and to live out my purpose. My attitude is that, "Whatever I put my mind to, I shall achieve it". Hence the title of my first book called 'Most People Only Try, I Make Sure'.

In 2004, I received an MBE for my work in the community. I was named Birmingham Young Professional of the Year in 2002 and Carlton TV's Business Midlander of the Year in 2003. I was also named Businessman of the Year for Black Businesses in Birmingham (3B's).

The secret to becoming successful is to find your gift. Discover what you are good at by asking yourself questions and then turning your gift into your biggest strength. Don't follow the crowd, be unique!

no more

eXcuses

Derek Browne

"saw my teenage years as a time for having fun, which meant there were periods of my life where I wasted my potential. I was the intelligent kid who chose to mess around at the back of the classroom; the class joker. The talent was all there, I just needed to be in the right place to bring it out.

eing the class joker and wanting to be one of the boys would not have helped me on my journey to date; a ccessful investment banker, an international athlete and now a social entrepreneur.

run a business called Entrepreneurs in Action (EiA). Our mission is to reduce the number of wasted talent in chools and to get young people from all backgrounds interested in entrepreneurship and employment"

The 'One Liner' Cheeky Kid

I was born in Tooting to strict West Indian parents. Did I appreciate their strictness? Of course not but looking back, it was very important in shaping who I am today.

At school I was what you would call the teachers' worst nightmare. I was a bright student but I did not feel comfortable with being in the top sets at school. I wanted to hang around with my friends in the lower groups.

At school I built up a reputation for having serious 'one liners' which often landed me in trouble. One of my teachers told me that I was going to be a postman because she couldn't see my potential, but I ignored her because I knew what I was going to be.

I left school with the O-levels I deserved but not with the O-levels I had the potential to achieve. I saw school as a place of fun and not as a place of learning, which meant I wasted my potential.

My advice to anyone still at school is to make the most out of the opportunity to learn, especially while education is free. Even if your friends are messing around or the teachers are ignoring you, you need to make sure that you work as hard as possible in order to leave school with good GCSE's because it will affect your future in a big way.

Friends....

Don't allow your friends to spoil your future. It wasn't until years after school that I realised friends are like lifts- they can either take you up or take you down. Hang on to friends who will take you up. You will know who they are because they want to achieve and will be pleased for you when you achieve.

Even though I messed around at school I was still able to get into college with my poor grades to study BTEC National Diploma in business and finance.

Eddie Murphy - 'My Trading Inspiration'

From the age of fourteen, I knew I wanted to be a trader after watching the Eddie Murphy film 'Trading Places'. I thought, "WOW, I can do that!" So after college I took up an A-level trainee's position at the Securities and Investments Board (now Financial Services Authority). At my interview I was able to get their agreement to allow me one day off a week to study for my HNC (Higher National Certificate) which was very similar to a degree qualification.

I soon realised that all the graduates were getting the great jobs, and one of the directors at my job encouraged me to do a degree. So off I went to study a business economics degree with law and accountancy at what is now known as London Metropolitan University.

Unable to get the work once I had graduated, after sending off 112 applications, I decided to take a job with Hays Recruitment Agency as a trainee. After eleven months there, I saw a job for a graduate position at Baring Brothers Bank so I went for it.

I took three days off to study for the interview and the test, and I learnt everything about Barings and the five people who ran the business. I got the job as a trader after eight interviews.

I became a trader after eighteen months. Upon reflection dreams can come true, but they only do when you put in the time and effort to achieve them.

To become a trader you don't necessarily need a degree; what employers look for is someone with determination, the right attitude and good qualifications.

No Limitations

I was not surprised that I became a trader because I knew I could do it. I never thought I should only apply for certain jobs because of my skin tone. I was not about to limit myself. I had the potential and the skills to be a good trader and that's all that mattered.

It's really not about race; it's all about your personality, attitude and what you have to offer to the company. Good traders need to be quick thinking, have good arithmetic skills and also be very courageous in times of challenge. I had all of those skills from when I was at school but I just did not know when and where to use them. With the right timing, confidence and vocabulary it was recognised as a personality within the boardroom.

International Athlete - Juggling Work And Athletics

While at Baring Brothers I was also competing for England in athletics. At the age of twenty five I became an international athlete in Triple Jump. People would ask me how I was able to do both. My motivation came from wanting to succeed. I didn't want to be one of those people who had the potential but never made it.

It was hard work but I knew that at the end of it I would get the results I wanted because I had put in all the work needed. I would go to work in the morning for around 7:00 am and then after work I would go straight to training for 7:00 pm. I trained six days a week and worked five days a week.

Sports Agent

After the closure of Barings Bank I followed one of my dreams to become a full-time entrepreneur. As a banker I often gave advice to fellow athletes on the trackside, so I then became an official sports agent to athletes like footballer Efan Ekoku and cricketer Chris Lewis and many more.

However I missed the buzz of city life. One day I received a call from Merrill Lynch, an investment bank, asking me to be a senior private banker for them, advising private clients on investments. They didn't have to ask me twice, I said, "yes" straight away. After a career spanning three decades in the city, I decided I needed a new challenge.

EiA

I realised that investment banking was not what I wanted to do anymore. What I really wanted to do was set up my own business doing something I was passionate about; working with young people. So in 2003, I set up Entrepreneurs in Action, a business aimed at teaching students the value of entrepreneurship and the mindset for entrepreneurial success.

The programs are designed to unlock the talents and to open the minds of the young people to the possibilities and opportunities in the business world. I wanted to provide a link between the world of business and education.

From The Classroom To The Boardroom

EiA run a number of programmes which provide students with a taste of real business. Our classroom to boardroom programme allows students to work on real life business challenges and present their solutions to senior directors in the boardroom. These programmes give students a sense of "real business".

We took a group of thirty six young people away to Cambridge University on an entrepreneurial camp for four days. They were not allowed to wear any hoodies or hats, or to use any street language. This was a place of work and we wanted to create an atmosphere to reflect that.

The experience was phenomenal as it really expended their minds and they ended up presenting to the chief executive of Barclays Bank in Canary Wharf.

On another project, we worked with over 200 school kids. We took them away in groups of thirty to complete different business challenges in an office based in the City of London for seven weeks. At the end of each week they had to present their results back to senior managers and directors in company boardrooms.

The aim of this project was to raise the aspirations of the students, to encourage them to engage in a more entrepreneurial way of thinking and to adopt an "I can do" attitude through a positive business experience.

Business

Your success in business is partly down to time management skills and having a great team around you who all have different strengths. Having a good team allows you to free up yourself to focus on what you do best.

If you have a business idea, write it down and then ask your friends and adults to critique your plans.

It's so important to be passionate about your business. It is not just about being motivated by money, it may be that you see a better way of providing a service or designing a product. Richard Branson did not chase money; he wanted to provide a better flying experience than British Airways when he set up Virgin Atlantic.

The Right Attitude

To be successful in life, you need to believe in yourself and what you can do. Once you have your self belief, determination and drive then you will be able to compete with everyone else in this world.

It's not about colour or the area you grew up in; it's all about your attitude, intelligence and willingness to learn. If you put in the hard work and remain persistent then you will overcome any barriers that come in your way.

As a social entrepreneur, my measure of success with EiA is the number of lives we inspire and change.

Think about what difference you can make!

no more

eXcuses

Lester Holloway

I was that kid who knew what I wanted to be from a young age; someone of influence. I was out there campaigning for my local wild life area from the age of fifteen. I was a bold little boy with passion, but I never knew that I would actually grow up and have a job that allowed me to bring about change.

w people read my articles and get to hear my opinions when they buy the New Nation, Britain's No.1 Black wspaper. So no more shouting on the streets, I can just write it, print it and then distribute it

Taking Responsibility

I grew up in Shepherds Bush with my parents and one sister. We used to move around a bit but we always lived in council flats or council houses. My parents both worked but it was painfully obvious that we were not rich because we used to walk around in second hand clothes, so I knew what it meant to struggle.

I was very quiet at school when I was younger. I did my work and disturbed no one, unlike some of the other black boys in my class.

I actually saw one of my class mates the other day begging on the streets around Shepherds Bush and it really upset me as it was obvious he was now on drugs.

I did notice while in school that there were groups of black boys who were allowed to drift to the back of the class and there was no real attempt by the teachers to re-engage them, so it was obvious that the next move for those boys was outside of the classroom.

Everyone has a part to play in life; teachers have their part to play towards your future, but the main responsibility falls on you. Even if the teacher has forgotten you, teach yourself to be the best because once you leave the school, the teacher will not care about your future.

Your excuse for failing cannot be, "The teacher ignored me", especially now that there are so many Saturday schools running and extra curriculum classes for black students.

Junior Politician

I studied English literature, history and art at college, but I actually ended up working in IT for a few years after I finished.

I then got into politics at a local level while I was still working in IT. I spent a four year term in politics but went full time for the last two terms as I was leading an organisation called the National Association of Black Councilors which took up a lot of my time.
I managed to survive financially but it was hard.

While I was a junior Politician I did a course on journalism. I wrote a lot of opinion pieces as a junior which I found quite easy to do and often received a lot of positive feedback from people about them. I realised that politics wasn't really for me, so I moved on and decided to do a degree in journalism at the University of East London (UEL).

The Media World

I was fortunate to find work experience at the New Nation and Hackney Gazette by contacting the editors of the newspapers but it was the Eastern Eye, an Asian newspaper that gave me my first job.

104

I worked there for seven months as a reporter. I then moved on to become a news editor at another Asian paper making sure I was learning all that I could about the industry, the ins and outs.

In my early years of journalism, I moved around working for quite a few different papers. I became a freelancer for the London Evening Standard, where the pay was rubbish but I loved the experience. My proudest feature while I was there was doing a double page spread on guns, and the business of converting guns. I also worked with the Sunday Telegraph.

Developing my skills further I went to work in radio and worked for BBC London. I was on their Community Affairs Unit, and developed black history month content for them. This was a good post as it was a topic I was interested in; researching about my people and talking about it.

I was also a reporter in 2003 for 5 Live. I was not afraid to try something new at all. I came to realise that employers were looking for people who were multi-skilled in a range of different areas such as web journalism, hard copy journalism or audio or visual journalism.

Average Journalist vs. Excellent Journalist

Attitude and determination are very important characteristics that employees look for in journalist. There will be many times when you will have to pitch your idea to the editor again and again before he will finally say, "Yes" but don't ever think that your story is not a story, it might just need to be tweaked or angled for that particular publication.

As a journalist, it's all about keeping your eyes open, reading widely, absorbing information and then processing it. You need to be on point; sniffing out stories everywhere you go, researching deep into subjects to give new knowledge to the readers.

The good thing about working in an office is that if you're bored with writing about news, you can easily walk over to another area in the office and make contacts with that department which could be fashion.

Contacts

This industry is all about who you know, that's how you really get promoted. Unfortunately there are not that many black journalists on national newspapers. Usually recommendations are made at dinner parties, which black people may not attend.

So if you want to work for a national paper you may have to work for free, just to get your foot onto the ladder. There's so much competition out there, so while you are there keep pitching your stories to the editor. Even if you get knocked back keep coming with new ideas because as long as you have ideas coming, you will definitely have a career in journalism.

Experience

A good way to learn how to write at the level of national papers is by looking at what the nationals do and the way they do it. Pick up the paper in the morning, look at the features through journalist eyes and then apply the principles that you learn from that style of writing or reporting to the story you want to do, so it becomes a story worth reading.

Another route into journalism is to work for local newspapers and work your way up. You need to believe that you will get that big break, that big story, that great article. I was lucky to go straight into the ethnic media so I didn't have to wait too long for a job, but if you continue to work hard and persevere then you will get recognised and promoted.

Before I became editor of the New Nation, Michael Eboda was editor for ten years. He decided to leave the New Nation to set up his own thing, so there was an opening for his job, anyone could go for the position, so I did as I knew my experience was right for this job.

I had been a freelance news reporter for years, I had worked as a news editor for a news website called Blink, I then became a news editor for The Voice newspaper and I was brought in as a senior reporter for a couple of months for the New Nation, so I was pretty confident.

I felt that I had worked hard over the years and had the skills to become that great editor that the New Nation were looking for, even though I knew it was not going to be easy.

Skills

As an editor I have to balance the whole process of the publication. I read all the features, look at the page set up, the whole lot, so it's important that I have an eye for detail.

Working at The Voice as a news editor was an excellent learning curve for me as it taught me a lot, so that I was able to do a great job at the New Nation. To be a great editor you need to have a good sense for news; knowing what the readers want to read week in and week out, but also you need to be able to edit people's work and know how to make it better.

To become a successful reporter or editor, you first need to believe in your ability. Research the audience of the paper and then hit them with a story that you know will keep them coming back.

As a journalist you look out for the stories, but as an editor you balance the whole newspaper; the personality of it, where it wants to get to, what issues you want to emphasise in your paper and what you want to avoid.

There is a historical, political and inspirational element behind the New Nation. We try not to be too victim centered but it's a bit hard as most of our calls are like that, and positive stories are harder to work on to make it readable, which means spending more time editing it, so it's my job to make sure we have the right balance.

Persistence

To get work experience, you just have to contact the editor of the magazine or newspaper, either by phone, email or any other way you can think off. It's best to meet with them and make a lasting impression.

I believe that if you want that big break you have to knock down every door that you can think of; every media outlet until someone opens it. You also need to make contacts and links; once someone knows who you are they will recommend you to their boss.

Someone Of Influence

Working now as the editor of the New Nation, Britain's No.1 selling black newspaper, with a readership of 60,000 is my dream job. I went from being that quiet boy in class to being someone of influence in the media industry.

It would have been easy for me to give up just like many others did when I was looking for that big break, but I persevered believing that I would make it.

My main motivation comes from wanting to make a difference in this world and my tool for bringing that about is through the media.

Tips on how to become successful:

1. Think like a winner
2. Change your attitude
3. Put 100% into everything you do
4. Surround yourself with people who want to be great, have dreams and aspirations
5. Despise illegal activities, have nothing to do with it
6. Value education, see the benefit of it
7. Allow yourself to be in a position to compete
8. Find people/ mentors who will invest in you and help you to get to your destination quicker
9. Learn from other peoples mistakes
10. See failure as a hitch along the path but not the end of the journey
11. Realise that the gold your looking for is in your mind
12. Take responsibility for your life, because no one else cares more than you
13. Speak a language the world can understand
14. Your past does not determine your future
15. Your greatness is linked to your purpose. Discovering your gift makes you unstoppable!
16. What you do today, does not only affect your tomorrow but your children's future.

by Sotonye Diri

Our Roots

CELEBRATING BLACK HISTORY

DID YOU KNOW....THAT THE MOST SUCCESSFUL BLACK ACTOR IN BRITAIN IS STILL **NORMAN BEATON** (1934-1994) OF THE DESMONDS FAME? THE LONG-RUNNING TV COMEDY WAS ENJOYED BY BOTH BLACK AND WHITE VIEWERS.

DID YOU KNOW...THAT BARONESS **PATRICIA SCOTLAND** Q.C. (1955-) IS THE FIRST BLACK FEMALE IN THE HOUSE OF LORDS AS WELL AS FIRST BLACK FEMALE BRITISH MINISTER?

DID YOU KNOW THAT...DREADLOCKED POET, WRITER AND PERFORMER **BENJAMIN ZEPHANIAH** (1958-) REFUSED TO BE HONOURED WITH THE ORDER OF THE BRITISH EMPIRE (OBE) BY HER MAJESTY THE QUEEN?

by TAJO FATUNLA

DID YOU KNOW...THAT ROLE MODEL, **JOANNE CAMPBELL** (1964-2002) ACTOR AND DRAMA THERAPIST WAS THE FIRST BLACK BRITISH ACTRESS TO PLAY ON STAGE, SARAH IN GUYS AND DOLLS?

DID YOU KNOW...THAT DR. **JOHN SENTAMU** (1949-) ARCHBISHOP OF YORK (2005) IS THE SECOND MOST POWERFUL LEADER IN THE CHURCH OF ENGLAND. BORN IN UGANDA, AFRICA, HE IS ENGLAND'S FIRST BLACK ARCHBISHOP.

DID YOU KNOW... THAT ONE OF BRITAIN'S OUTSTANDING POST SECOND WORLD WAR BLACK SCULPTORS WAS **RONALD MOODY** (1900-1984)? HIS BIGGEST COMMISSIONED PIECES WAS FOR THE JAMAICAN GOVERNMENT.

DID YOU KNOW...THAT **LORIE BLACKMAN** IS THE [MO]ST SUCCESSFUL FEMALE [BL]ACK BRITISH AUTHOR FOR [C]HILDREN IN BRITAIN? HER [WR]ITINGS ALLOWED HER TO [P]UT BLACK CHILDREN INTO BOOKS SO THAT THEY [CO]ULD RELATE TO STORIES SHE WROTE.

DID YOU KNOW...THAT THE FIRST BLACK PERSON'S LIFE STORY TO BE KNOWN IN BRITAIN WAS THAT OF SEAMAN, **BRITON HAMMON**? HE LIVED IN GREENWICH, SOUTH EAST LONDON. HE COULD NOT READ OR WRITE SO HE DICTATED HIS LIFE HISTORY FOR PUBLICATION.

www.tayofatunla.com

Ken Barnes Character Profile Questionnaire

Welcome to Ken Barnes Character Profile Questionnaire. This questionnaire is meant to help you determine some aspects of your character. It is not meant to be used as a diagnostic tool, but rather as a tool to give you insight into parts of your character that may be having a negative impact on your life.

Please note that this is not a scientifically validated questionnaire

Questions are answered by placing the number you feel correctly reflects your thoughts next to each question.

```
1   2   3   4   5
|   |   |   |   |
'N' 'L' 'S' 'M' 'A'
```

ANSWER KEY:
'N' No/ Never
'L' Not really / As little as possible
'S' Sometimes
'M' Most of the time
'A' Yes/ Always

Expectations

1. _____ Do you feel that your teachers expect you to do well in your education?

2. _____ Do you feel that your parents expect you to do well in life?

3. _____ Do you believe that you will live a better life than your parents did?

4. _____ Do you think you will be able to get a good job?

5. _____ When you look at yourself in the mirror, do you only see your good points?

6. _____ Are you strong enough to not let other people's opinions of you affect the way you feel about yourself?

7. _____ Do you believe that you are capable of achieving great things in your life?

E: Score _____ (Add up the total score)

The character profile questionnaire and action plan has been taken from
Ken Barnes book- 'The Seven Principles of Respectisms Workbook'- www.kenbarnes.co.uk

Time

1. _____ Are you always on time for appointments?

2. _____ Do you believe that what you do not do today cannot always be done another day?

3. _____ Do you believe that being late is disrespectful?

4. _____ Do you always use you time in the best possible way?

5. _____ Do you believe that if someone is five minutes late for a lesson each time, it can affect the grade he/she gets from that lesson?

6. _____ Are deadlines of real importance to you?

7. _____ Do you do your best to complete a task on time?

T: Score _____ (Add up your total score)

Education

1. _____ Do you get on with most of your teachers?

2. _____ Do you find education satisfying because it gives you a sense of accomplishment?

3. _____ Do you think your education is the best chance for you to succeed in life?

4. _____ Would you like to be considered smart or a nerd?

5. _____ How often do you put as much energy and enthusiasm as you can into your education?

6. _____ How often do you try to be the first one in class to answer questions?

7. _____ Do you look forward to going to school to learn?

E: Score _____ (Add up your total score)

The character profile questionnaire and action plan has been taken from Ken Barnes book- 'The Seven Principles of Respectisms Workbook'- www.kenbarnes.co.uk

Expectations

(Score of 0-15) You do not have many expectations for your life. You believe that your parents or teachers do not expect much from you either. At times you do not feel good about yourself and allow other peoples opinions to dictate how you feel. Remember, everybody is unique and has special gifts. You do as well, but you just need to find them. Look deeper into yourself and you will find your talent.

(Score of 16-27) You have some expectations for yourself, but get disillusioned easily. You believe that you might have a good future; however, the belief you have in yourself is dictated too much by other people and not yourself. Repeat to yourself 'I am going to be somebody' as often as you can.

(Score of 28-35) You have high expectations of yourself. You believe in your ability to succeed in life. You feel very good about yourself and will not let other people's opinions of you affect you in a negative way. Life is full of opportunities and you are going to go after them all.

Time

(Score of 0-15) Most of the time you are late for your appointments. You do not consider being on time to be that important. You procrastinate as you believe that what you do not do today can always be done another day. Always leave more time than you need to help you avoid being late.

(Score of 16-27) You try to make the best use of your time but it does not always work out. You need to slow down and not take on so many things. Start practicing being ten minutes early for your appointments or finishing your tasks way before the deadlines.

(Score of 28-35) You are someone who is always on time. You understand that once time is lost it doesn't come back. As such, you aim to make the best use of the time you have. You consider lateness disrespectful and inconsiderate. You also like to plan ahead.

The character profile questionnaire and action plan has been taken from
Ken Barnes book- 'The Seven Principles of Respectisms Workbook'- www.kenbarnes.co.uk

Education

(Score of 0-15) You do not really enjoy education. For you, learning is something you have to do rather than something you want to do and if you can avoid it you will. You find school/college boring and normally can't wait for the day to end. Start recognising that your education is your ticket to a better life and then you will value your education more.

(Score of 16-27) You turn up to school/college everyday but you do not always put as much effort in as you should. You know you need a good education; however, you get easily distracted at times. You need to focus more and not get distracted. Changing where you sit in class might help eliminate distractions.

(Score of 28-35) You value education. You work hard at school/college and want to get a good education. You do not mind being seen as a nerd or smart as you believe that a good education will give you greater choices in your life and career.

Wisdom Quotes

"A mind once stretched by a new idea never regains its original dimensions"
Anonymous

"I CAN is 100 times more important than IQ"
Anonymous

"LOST time is never found again"
Benjamin Franklin

"Procrastination is the thief of time"
Edward Young

The character profile questionnaire and action plan has been taken from en Barnes book- 'The Seven Principles of Respectisms Workbook'- www.kenbarnes.co.uk

Ken Barnes Action Plan

Use this section of the book to develop your character building goals. Do not miss out on this section because hope is merely a dream. When you envision your plan and schedule it, your dream can become a reality.

A= Action you are going to take
R= Reason for taking action
D= Date you will be taking action

Expectations

A

R

D

Time

A

R

D

The character profile questionnaire and action plan has been taken from Ken Barnes book- 'The Seven Principles of Respectisms Workbook'- www.kenbarnes.co.u

Education

A

R

D

The character profile questionnaire and action plan has been taken from
Ken Barnes book- 'The Seven Principles of Respectisms Workbook'- www.kenbarnes.co.uk

My Story and Acknowledgments

When I was younger, if anyone ever told me that something was impossible, I made sure I proved to them that it was possible. I never allowed anyone to make me believe that I was limited in life because of my skin tone or my family background. We were all created with unique features and have different personalities, different strengths and areas we need to work on, but no one has more of an excuse than any other person! Find the best way that works for you!

My Biggest Role Model

My mum has always been a very positive woman. Even though we may not have had all the material things like other families, she showed us unconditional love. I grew up in a Christian home and we were taught to have faith in God. My mum would always pray and sing around the house.

Even though I was born In England, I was very aware of my culture especially when it came to education. As a Nigerian you were expected to study but not just study, study hard!

I remember we used to have a math's teacher called Mr. Kofi who would come to the house once a week. My mum did not have a lot of money but she always made sure that whatever she had she invested it into mine and my sibling's education. She sacrificed so much for us, just so we could have a great start in life.

Knowing that made me even more determined to want to do well at school, I wanted to make my mum proud of me so she would know that all the sacrifices she had made for me were not in vain.

My mum worked very hard to ensure that we had everything that we needed. We always had food to eat and clothes to wear even though they may not have always been designer. I remember when my mum brought me no-name trainers; I wore them to school and one boy laughed at me. It wasn't until year 6 of primary school that I finally got my first pair of designer trainers.

My mum taught me how to save my money and how to be appreciative of everything we had in life, be it big or small.

Independence - The Yellow Trolley

At the age of twelve I started a newspaper round which I did for three years. I used to spend Friday nights watching 'Top of the Pops' while putting the leaflets into the newspapers, and then on Saturday morning I would be up by 8:00am to distribute them.

I was so embarrassed because I had a big ugly yellow trolley to pull behind me and I thought I was doing a boy's job. Surprisingly none of my friends laughed at me.

It was at this young age that I learnt about independence. I learnt that if I wanted to buy things I had to work for it because I didn't want to constantly be asking my mum for money. I was earning about £5.00 a week for delivering 150 newspapers plus leaflets. I learnt how to save this money and look after myself.

Life Can Be Unfair

At school I was well behaved but I did talk a lot. I was in all the top sets and I never missed a day of school until the final year of secondary school, two weeks before we went on study leave.

I was called into my deputy heads office and told that I was being sent on early study leave due to an incident that had occurred with some of my friends and another girl. I had never been in trouble at school before, nor received any warnings for misbehaviour, so this was truly unfair.

I couldn't believe it, but I chose not to get bitter. A lot of my teachers felt sorry for me and met up with me after school to go over the lessons I had missed. They could see how much I wanted to do well and I came out with the second highest GCSE grades in my year and the highest grades out of the girls; 4a*, 4a's and 4b's.

If I had decided to get angry and give up I would have messed up my own future and life would have been a lot harder for me but I chose to turn the situation into a positive one and started my revision early.

My Big Sister

While at secondary school and college my big sister was a great role model as she set a good example for me to follow. She studied hard and did well. People used to think that I was so intelligent but it was really because my sister helped me.

When I was sixteen years old my sister fell pregnant, she was only 18. Many people tried to say that she was going to become another statistic; a young mother with no real qualifications but she proved them all wrong.

Even with a little child to care for, she was working, went onto university at the age of 20, and gradated with a psychology degree, getting a 1st for her dissertation (a very long essay). She then secured a well paid job with Pfizer, the top pharmaceutical company in the world as a Medical Representative.

My sister taught me one of life's greatest lessons; you don't have to accept other peoples labels if you know who you are.

The Balance

From a young age I have always tried to get the right balance. I used to make my friends Jolene and Tamika go to the library with me and then we would go on our bus rides to Trocadero afterwards. I knew that if I wanted to do well in life, I had to get the balance right between fun and work.

I remember at Sir George Monoux College my English teacher, Mr. Bond saying to me, "How is it that you're able to be so popular and still be at the top of the class?" I saw being intelligent, as being more attractive and fun then being dumb and stupid. I was not one of those girls who turned up to college, just to hang in the canteen.

At college, I was encouraged to apply for Oxford University and I got called for an interview. One of my older friends Amma had gotten into Oxford and she encouraged me to go for it. She helped me with my personal statement and my application form but I never got in, however I was very happy that I had applied because I now believed that anything was possible.

Church

At the age of fifteen I was fortunate enough to start attending a church around the corner from my house called Christian Life City which changed my life. I was taught how to develop myself personally, by reading great books like the Bible and other self-help books on positive mental attitude. The preaching I heard from my Bishop Wayne Malcolm taught me how to be the best I can be, which formed my foundation for later on in life!

Friends

While at Queen Mary University I met three amazing girls called Chierika, Becky and Jennifer who showed me true friendship. Chierika taught me the importance of keeping a diary and introduced me to the word 'entrepreneur'. Becky always encouraged me to be confident and to believe in my ability, while Jennifer always prayed for me and encouraged me with her wise words.

Through out my life I have always had positive people around me; Abike, Mary, Nikki, Sabrina, Paul, Joshua, David, Robert and Tunde. They all believed in me, and encouraged me in whatever I wanted to do.

Abike and Sabrina taught me how to be strong in difficult situations by always remaining positive and having faith. Tunde taught me the art of communication and good time management skills. Joshua, David and Paul always knew what to say if I needed that extra encouragement and Nikki and Mary showed me true friendship.

Mentors

In my life I have been very blessed to have met some amazing men and women who have become my mentors; Jackson, Jenniffer, Susan and Karen. They all believed in me and gave me an opportunity to learn and grow by throwing me in at the deep end with no floats. They brought out the best in me, especially at times when I wanted to be lazy or I lacked confidence.

My business mentor Len and also my youth pastor, made me believe that no one is ever too young to get into business. He supported me and gave me hope when times got really hard. Having wonderful mentors in your life is key to your growth and success, especially if they've been where you're going.

No More Excuses

When I had the idea for this great book 'No More Excuses', even before I started to contact the role models, one of the first people I ever told was a young lady called Mildred. I needed guidance and she was the right person for the job. Mildred invested her time into me without asking for anything back and gave me the hope I needed to believe that everything would work out.

During the writing of 'No More Excuses', I was able to depend on my friends, Jennifer, Abike, Becky, Storme, and Marsha for help. If it wasn't for them the process would have been a lot harder.

Also the initial support I received from Jaleesa, Shikira, Khadijah, Chantelle and Anthony was what really kept me going. They believed in 'No More Excuses' when it was still an idea.

Most of all, I would like to thank all the 16 role models in this book. Thank you for making time out for me to interview you but most of all, thank you for living a life that the readers of this book can aspire to.

A big thank you also to all of those that contributed to the content of this book; Ken, Tayo and MIA publishers.

Mixture

So as you can see, my life has been shaped by those listed above and many others. They have all contributed to my success and who I am today, a positive young lady who believes that there are 'NO MORE EXCUSES'.

'BELIEVE in your dreams
and they may come true;
BELIEVE in yourself
and they WILL COME TRUE'

Anonymous

'NO MORE EXCUSES,
MAKE IT HAPPEN'

Jackson Ogunyemi

Lightning Source UK Ltd.
Milton Keynes UK
27 July 2010

157458UK00002B/26/P